**Confessions From a Recruiter:
Career Advice, Stories and a Spine Tingling Plot
Twist**

Acknowledgements

Melissa Rowell: Thank you for your excellent editing work! I appreciate all of the attention to detail and the fact that you will have read this book more times than anyone else ever will!

Katie Labedz: Thank you for all of your advice, support, mentorship and encouragement! I wouldn't be where I am today without your guidance. You keep me grounded and I am forever grateful.

Dave: Thanks for your support and putting up with all of my Unicorn games. There's no one else that could handle me the way that you do. I don't know how you do it but I love and appreciate you for all that you do!

Table of Contents

Confessions From a Recruiter
Career Advice, Stories, and a Spine Tingling Plot Twist

Introduction

One of the most stressful aspects of our lives involves finding a new job, and we will all find ourselves changing jobs, or even changing careers, multiple times over the course of our lives. Job searches can be rewarding when we find the right job, but they can also be stressful and frustrating.

I've worked as a recruiter for staffing agencies and corporations both globally and domestically. One thing that is consistent across the board is that everyone wants to know what the best method is for getting that dream job. What is the right resume format? Do I need a cover letter? Why am I not getting interviews or offers?

As a career and leadership coach I work with people who are trying to secure their next role or move up the ladder in their current organization. It's rewarding to watch people secure their next gig or promotion, but it's heartbreaking to watch people struggle through the job search. There's so much information out there, and everyone has a different opinion about what's right and what's not. A simple internet search will bring up a ton of articles and many contradict the others. What's a job seeker to do? Who should you follow?

I've set the layout of this book to mirror the recruiting life cycle. From finding a recruiter and applying to onboarding and starting your new job. Each process is different depending on the level of a position that you're applying to, the company, and the interview team. Not all companies and recruiters operate the same so always leverage your network and resources when you're job searching. This is designed to be one resource for you.

My company is called Unicorn Recruitment & Career Services because I've heard over and over and over again in my career that the hiring manager wanted that *Unicorn*. The candidate who hit all the marks and glittered and sparkled and rode in on a rainbow. As a recruiter, I'd know my candidates could do the job. They could do it 200% and would give it their all. They could be the superstar. But something in the interview was off. Or something on their resume seemed inconsistent or it didn't stand out. I created my company to help people become the unicorns that managers wanted to see. The unicorns that they thought that they needed. Ultimately, we can all be unicorns. It's about positioning ourselves well, selling ourselves, and sharing our best attributes.

I combine my years of recruiting with leadership coaching to help people not only find new positions, but to help others climb that corporate ladder. I want everyone to learn how to become the best versions of themselves so that their careers are in their hands, not their employer's or manager's.

This book is designed to help you through your career search, but also to provide a bit of entertainment and perspective as to what the other side of the job search is like. Perhaps sharing some insight into the hiring process from a recruiter's perspective will help you on your journey. Whatever your career path, I hope this advice will help you navigate the waters of the job search.

Chapter 1: The Love/Hate Relationship with Recruiters

A few searches on LinkedIn, and you can find plenty of business professionals detailing all the reasons that they don't like working with recruiters. Throughout the course of my career I've been told that I'm a necessary evil more times than I can count. However, you can also find people singing their recruiter's praises when they score a job. You can find recruiters advocating for their candidates and trying to find them the best possible deal. But there are also recruiters who you never hear from and are relatively silent on social media.

The terms 'ghosting' and 'bait and switch' come up quite often when people are talking about their experiences with recruiters. Ghosting refers to when a recruiter stops following up with a candidate and stops responding to their messages. Bait and switch means that they told you the job details were different than what they actually were, and the candidate finds out the real scope of the role or salary later on in the interview process.

Job seekers often share their frustrations about recruiters or employers who don't follow up, interview processes that take too long, lack of feedback, or the aspects of the job being very different from what they originally applied to. Right or wrong, recruiters take the brunt of the frustration and blame for inefficient processes or vague feedback.

There are certainly some recruiters that aren't responsive and drop the ball. However, I hope to shed some light on what goes on behind the scenes and maybe answer some of the questions that every job seeker has asked themselves.

So Why the Extremes? The Difference Between Agency and Corporate Recruiters

There's a large difference between agency recruiters and corporate recruiters. Staffing agency recruiters make their living by cultivating relationships with business professionals. Whether they have a job that's a fit for you or not, they hang onto your information so they have a network of people to reach out to when a new position rolls in. They work for a variety of different businesses and are measured by how many people they network with and how many positions they fill. This means that agency recruiters are responsible for reaching out to potential candidates and finding people who are interested in, or may be interested in, a new position in the future.

Corporate recruiters are part of the internal talent acquisition team and work for the company that they are employed with. Their job is to find the right people for the company, and their loyalty is to the company versus the candidates. That's not to say they don't advocate for the candidates who they think are a good fit for the role, but ultimately, they don't work for the candidate.

As an internal recruiter, I would push for the candidate that I thought was the best cultural and technical fit; however, I wasn't the final decision maker. I worked for the hiring manager, and they ultimately made the decision. Even when I knew they were making the wrong hiring choice, I could voice my opinion, document my disagreement with the hiring manager and sit back and let the pieces fall into place.

Just like any other profession, there are people who are great at their jobs and others who aren't. If you're reading this and thinking, but I've worked with agency recruiters who didn't call me back, you aren't alone. Agency recruiters are often assigned to several requisitions at a time and need to work on the next 'hot' requisition as soon as it comes in. It's a fast paced, competitive environment. Not only are they competing with the other recruiters in their office, but they're also competing with other staffing agencies if the company has called it out to multiple recruiters. Since they're often paid a relatively low base salary, they are forced to live on the commission earned when they fill a position. This means they drop anything that's not profitable and focus on where there's potential for commission. Unfortunately, that means that follow ups with unsuccessful candidates is sometimes low on the priority list.

Agency recruiters don't always have direct contact with a client either, sometimes working through a vendor management system or a third party for feedback. It doesn't make it right, but I've seen agency recruiters ghost candidates after they've been ghosted by a client. They don't have any feedback so the position becomes out of sight, out of mind. It's an unfortunate product of a competitive industry.

Corporate recruiters have a slightly different recruiting process. Once a position is approved, a corporate recruiter posts a position on the company website and job boards. Depending on the role and the recruiter, they may or may not do their own outreach. Larger, well-known companies tend to receive more direct applicants than smaller companies without the brand recognition meaning that their in-house recruiters are less likely to need to do outreach.

When I worked internally, we did outreach and actively sourced (looked for candidates), but it was all dependent on the amount of time and the requisition workloads we had. Often we would do an initial search and campaign for candidates, and then spend the next week or two fielding responses and interviewing candidates. Once we had a few candidates, the outreach activity had to stop because we had multiple requisitions on our desk, and we had to move onto roles where we didn't have candidates.

When agency recruiters move from their agency to an in-house role, you typically see that they are more likely to reach out and network with talent to fill positions. It's how they are trained, and it's part of their process.

Corporate recruiters not only post jobs and do phone screens, they are also responsible for Diversity, Equity, and Inclusion Practices, Equal Employment

Opportunity and recruiting metrics reporting, applicant tracking system improvements, process improvements, career events, and managing multiple different hiring managers. They often are carrying requisition workloads of 20+. My all time high was 87 requisitions. All of this extra work not only stretches them thin, but it contributes to their buy-in and loyalty to the company that they work for. They aren't just recruiters, they're talent attraction specialists and are a part of the company's overall talent strategy.

When a hiring manager declines to move forward with a candidate, the recruiter is responsible for notifying the declined candidate(s). Most often this comes in the form of an auto-decline email with little feedback as to why the candidate was not selected. Another search on social media, and you'll find that quite a few people would like detailed feedback on why they weren't selected.

There are a lot of reasons why candidates aren't selected. An internal candidate applied, a referral candidate came through, there were numerous candidates and someone else was technically stronger, the position was canceled, or the position was put on hold. And one of those reasons that a recruiter will very rarely tell you: you didn't interview well and bombed the interview. An in-house recruiter is not going to tell you what you didn't do well. This is tough to hear, but it's not their job or place and some companies have policies on the type of feedback that they give to external candidates. A corporate recruiter is there to find the best candidate for their company, and they have to move on once they've decided for or against a candidate.

If you're working with an agency recruiter, they may receive more detailed feedback from a client and share areas of improvement with you so you know for your next interview. Some corporate recruiters will share more details about why you weren't selected, but it's a different relationship than you might have with an agency recruiter, so don't take it personally if you don't receive the feedback you want.

Ok, so now you know the difference between the types of recruiters, and you probably know that an agency recruiter can be an ally for you. But how do you find a good recruiter?

Finding the Right Recruiter

The first thing that I would recommend is networking with several recruiters. They work with different clients and different industries, and you can widen your reach by working with several recruiters. Recruiters are your allies in the career search, but they're working with multiple candidates so why shouldn't you work with multiple recruiters? Recruiters may not like this advice, but I've always advised candidates to work with several, high quality recruiters. When I know others in my field or industry, I often recommend several other recruiters to the candidates that I'm working with as well.

Next, find recruiters that specialize in your industry and profession. Recruiters usually have a niche in the industry, meaning that they work within healthcare, manufacturing, technology, etc. Within those industries you can break down the specialty even further and find recruiters that specialize in just nursing recruiting or just software engineering roles. These recruiters are going to have the best grasp on the market and your skill set. I've focused on manufacturing, technology, healthcare, and corporate roles. I am much more comfortable talking about a candidate's experience when I understand their skill set and the industry that they work in. I would not be equipped to effectively sell a candidate to a client in the banking or insurance industries. I'd give it my best effort, but a recruiter that focuses on those industries and professions would be a much safer bet. Recruiters that tell you they can do it all maybe can, but not to the degree that an industry expert can.

Throughout my career I've spoken with candidates that I just can't help. I can give them advice, help with a resume, and coach them on interviews, but they aren't in my field of expertise. I've passed them along to other recruiters who can better help them. Ask colleagues or friends who they've used, search for specific recruiters in your industry, and network on LinkedIn to find the right recruiter for you.

Lastly, in my experience, going to one of the large staffing companies may be ok for early on in your career, but once you're more established it's best to look for a smaller boutique firm with experienced recruiters. Recruiting is a tough industry. The turnover is high. I've trained numerous recruiters over the years, and the ones that make it past the first few years are typically in it for the long haul. I'm not saying steer clear of all of the big name firms, but I am saying to look into who you're working with. Someone who is six months into their recruiting career isn't going to be equipped to help a senior level professional move into a leadership role. They may also not be with the company or even still recruiting six months from now, and then you have to start again.

Look for someone who is responsive and isn't trying to push you into every role that comes across their desk. I have had roles I was struggling to find candidates for that have been open for over a year. When I had the perfect candidate in front of me, but they didn't want to relocate and certainly didn't want to drive over an hour one way to work each day, I had to let them decline. It hurts and it's painful, but a good recruiter should be able to talk through your situation with you as a person, and not push you into something that isn't going to be the right fit for you.

How to Leverage Your Recruiter

Ok, great. You've found a few agency recruiters that you feel good about and engage with them. So how does this all work?

Recruiters will want to get to know you. They want to hear about your background, your skill set, what types of roles you're looking for, and what your career goals are. These are great people to leverage if you have questions regarding your industry, the job market, or what companies are hiring and looking for. Prepare questions for them about your search, and set time aside to meet with them. Too often candidates forgot that an informal call with me was still kind of an interview. Candidates who called me while they were out on a run or grocery shopping weren't focused, they gave me distracted answers, and they weren't invested in our conversation. Things don't always go as planned, and people have had to call me while stuck in traffic or talk to me in a low voice because they had ducked into a closet at work. Life happens, but try to invest in the conversation because the recruiter needs to know all about you and your skill set if they're going to help you.

Next, make sure you're giving them the total picture. The who, what, why, when, where, and how about your background and where you want to be. Good recruiters have a sixth sense about people, and we can read between the lines and come to conclusions, but we are not mind readers. With today's various work environments and rising inflation, people are more focused on work expectations and benefits than ever before. Which is great! But, just make sure that you give your recruiter specifics.

For example, I had a candidate who told me they would only do remote. Not hybrid. Not onsite. 100% remote. So I only considered them for roles that were remote. They called me one day and asked if I was working on a job at a specific company because they had seen a post that I had made. I confirmed that I was, and they were hurt and angry that I didn't consider them. The role was hybrid, three days onsite and two days remote. I had asked them previously if there were any conditions where they would consider a hybrid role, and they had adamantly said no.

The company was down the street from their neighborhood, and they could walk there. They could still get home in time to get kids off the bus from school or run home on lunch. This was a lesson learned for both of us. I now ask multiple, multiple times: What conditions would you consider onsite or hybrid? If the company was in your backyard? If it's a big name company? What company would you love to work at regardless of whether it's onsite, hybrid, or remote?

It's also ok if something changes when you're searching for a job. Just give your recruiter a heads up. You decide you want to go onsite. Ok, no problem. You're moving now, and your geographical target area is changing. Got it. You would do anything to work for X company. We can do that. Interviewing at another company through another recruiter or on your own? Good luck, and let me know if you need interview tips!

Communication is key when working with a recruiter. Give them updates on your career search and things that are changing in your world, and they'll do the same.

Chapter 2: Recruiter Experience Stories

Everyone remembers the extremes, the best of the best and the worst of the worst. Recruiters are no exception. When it comes to the candidates that I've worked with over the years, the ones that stand out the most to me are the ones that were truly amazing experiences as well as the ones that made me rethink my profession.

Let's start with the time I almost ran from recruiting full speed without looking back.

I was a relatively junior recruiter, only a few years in, and I had someone who I was working with for a senior level technical position. I spoke with the candidate on the phone, we had met in person at my office, and we had been talking for a few months while I was keeping an eye out for roles for him. He was gainfully employed and the next step was going to be a higher level position for him so he wasn't ready to just jump for anything and everything that came along.

I shared a leadership position with him and went through the details. It would be a relocation, but he was ok with it, and it was in a city that he was willing to move to for the right opportunity. We discussed the pay and full benefits. He knew their timeline and that they were actively hiring, but that they had internal and external candidates in play, and he knew it was going to be a process. We talked through the role and the what if's for hours over several conversations.

He agreed that he was ready to submit his application and move forward with the position. I get his submittal package together and send it over to my client with a long email about why he's a great candidate and ask them to set up an interview with him right away.

An hour later I had an email from the hiring manager at my client: Call me.

Anyone that has had a manager or client tell them to call them right away, without further details, knows that sinking feeling in your stomach. I hoped he wanted to set up an interview, but I knew this manager, and if he did want to interview my candidate he would have sent me times to book on his calendar.

I took a deep breath and picked up the phone (we still had desk phones at this time). The manager was kind because I knew him, but the story he told me was not like anything I could have prepared myself for.

The candidate had interviewed with this company for another role a year ago. He had applied directly, and they had agreed that he looked great on paper. The internal recruiter had phone screened him, he had done a phone call, and one of his peers had done a phone call with this candidate as well. They brought him in for a final onsite interview, and that's where it derailed.

The candidate had asked to fly in for the interview versus driving three hours. They had agreed because he was from a larger city and didn't have a car. When he arrived at the airport, the internal recruiter arranged that he would pick him up. The recruiter went above and beyond because not many recruiters have time to pick candidates up from the airport! The entire drive to the office, the candidate complained about the flight, and then ridiculed the recruiter for how he was driving, and the fact that the recruiter had picked a bad flight/arrival time because they were fighting traffic.

Ok, we've all been there, right? Bad travel arrangements, anxiety. Well…

This candidate had been asked to prepare some technical assignments for this particular interview process. The first part of the interview was with the technical team to go over how he approached the case studies they had given him. He looked at the team and told them, "I'm not doing free work here so I didn't complete them. If you want me to do them now, I will, but you're going to have to pay me."

These were not projects that the team was working on. These were assessments and scenario based questions to get a better understanding of his technical depth and ability to problem solve. This had been explained to him, and I had looked at them as well. I can promise you this client was not looking for free project work (I've had others that have so it does happen!).

The candidate rounded out the interview by making a sexist comment to the HR Manager and telling the hiring manager that in three years, he saw himself taking over the hiring manager's job and firing the team so he could start over and rebuild the team from the ground up.

I had interviewed quite a few people by this point in my career, and when I tell you I never saw this coming, I mean it! This candidate didn't give me any indication of these behaviors. He knew he had interviewed with this team. He knew that he didn't get the role, and that he had voiced his displeasure about the interview process to the hiring manager and recruiter.

WHY WOULD HE WANT TO INTERVIEW WITH THEM AGAIN?!

Why didn't he tell me?

Any guesses on what he had to say when I called him?

He told me that he didn't think I needed to know he had interviewed there in the past because I didn't submit him for that role.

When I asked him why he was still interested in the role after he had told the hiring team the previous year that he wanted the job so he could fire them all, he first tried telling me that he was just really interested in the company. Then when I wasn't buying it he finally told me he wanted to see what would happen if he got an interview with them. He thought that I would take his name off the resume, and they would want to interview him. He wanted to see the looks on their faces when he walked in for the interview again.

What?!

This professional, who I had worked with for months and had multiple conversations with, had lunch with several times, wanted to see the shock on their faces when he showed up for an interview again. He wanted them to feel uncomfortable for not hiring him the last time.

And when I asked him about berating the internal recruiter, he confessed he just simply didn't like the guy that much. That was it. When I asked for clarification about telling the hiring manager that he wanted his job so he could fire the team, he simply said: "Well, someone needed to tell them they were inept."

Yikes.

I still have trauma from this experience. I submit candidates with one eye open, and it takes a while before I fully trust candidates. If you're wondering why recruiters are hammering you with the same questions and asking repeatedly if you've ever crossed the street in front of the company that they're submitting you to… this is why!

If you're wondering if I ever worked with that candidate again, I sure did not. We ended that call parting ways with me telling him he would need to find a new recruiter to work with. Recruiters absolutely mark people DNUs (do not use), and that candidate was marked with a big red flag in my notes. He may very well be an excellent professional, but recruiters stake their reputations on the professionalism of the candidates who they submit. I couldn't submit him in good conscience anywhere, and I'd never trust that he hadn't submitted himself already, or behave poorly when being interviewed.

This could have been avoided if he had explained to me the situation of his candidacy the previous year. I would have had a conversation with the hiring manager regarding what happened, asking if he would reconsider him if my candidate was truly interested in the position and if he was aware of how he had lacked professionalism the last time.

Not all candidates do this, right?

Right. Most are great to work with and many of my professional friends are people I hired or worked with as candidates at one point of time or another.

One of my favorite stories is a candidate that I worked with for a relatively short amount of time, but with high success, and we've stayed in contact over the years, allowing me to watch her grow in her career.

This particular candidate had been applying for months without so much as a call back. She had a very niche technical skill set, and I knew she was in demand so I was surprised to hear that she hadn't landed a job. This sends a recruiter's spidey sense up. Her resume needed some work, but with her tech experience I knew companies and other recruiters would look past that.

I met with her in person to get a better understanding of how she was presenting herself. When I met her she was professionally dressed, complete with a padfolio, and business suit even though she was meeting with a recruiter in a coffee shop. We dove into her background and her experience. She was on a work visa and asked me if I thought that was preventing her from landing a role. Knowing the companies that she was applying to; it wouldn't have prevented her from getting a new role as they frequently sponsored visas.

I asked her to walk me through her interviews. What were they asking her, and how was she responding? Here's where we figured out what was going on.

She told me that while she could understand most of the questions asked of her, she was still learning English and she was struggling with conveying her experience at times. We talked about reasonable accommodations and what that could mean for her when she was interviewing. She didn't know she could ask for an interpreter.

We had an open role at one of our clients, and I cleaned up her resume, sent it to the recruiter, and let them know we would need an interpreter. They arranged an interpreter for the interview. We made an offer to her the same day.

This woman cried and thanked me profusely. She only had weeks left on her visa, and this job ensured she could stay in the country. I did nothing out of the ordinary, not even above and beyond, but sometimes it's just a matter of being in someone's corner that makes the difference. In this case, being in her corner meant asking a few questions to seek clarification rather than declining her because of a language barrier.

We've kept in contact over the years, and she's now on her green card and is at an architect level. Since this candidate was so forthcoming with her situation and what she was experiencing, I was able to be a resource for her rather than just another recruiter that tossed her resume around.

It's not always this easy, but most of the time, communication can resolve a lot of the issues you're having with recruiters or in your job search!

Chapter 3: The Perfect Portfolio!

You've updated your resume, you've written a cover letter and now you're applying!

But where are the interviews?

Here's the deal with resumes and cover letters. You can ask 100 recruiters what their preferred resume format is, and you will get 100 different answers. There isn't a one size fits all resume. You won't please everyone. There is no way.

However, what you can do is put together a clean and easy to read resume that won't cause any issues or spark attitude from those more difficult recruiters out there. There may be resumes that come across my desk that aren't necessarily my favorite layout, but they aren't offensive so I review them. (And yes, there are offensive resumes out there!) You have six seconds of the recruiter's attention. A corporate recruiter is scanning a few key pieces of your resume, and if they have to navigate unnecessary information, they're going to move on.

As I mentioned before, every recruiter has their preference so these are my preferences based on feedback I've received from other recruiters.

What You Should Absolutely Not Do on Your resume!

References or 'References Upon Request'.

It's just not needed anymore. No one is going to call your references without at the very least talking to you first. Most reference checks come after an offer is made and with most companies not being willing to verify anything more than employment dates and rehire eligibility information, references are becoming an outdated hiring practice.

In all of my years of hiring, I only had one bad reference check, and it wasn't *bad.* The manager just hadn't supervised the candidate long enough to give me much feedback. As a recruiter, I know that no one is going to give me a reference who didn't like them. No one.

No candidate is ever going to say, here's my manager, they hated me and fired me, but you can call them. Even if they did, that manager is going to be careful about what they say because they don't want a lawsuit or to be fired from their job.

So the fact that we don't really take credence in references, and they aren't done usually until after an offer is made means they just don't need to be on your resume. They're taking up valuable space. I don't need your reference's contact information. I need to know why you're a fit for the job.

If you have an online portfolio of your work, that is more valuable than references, and it takes up less space!

Political or Religious Affiliations, Hobbies, Interests

There are some recruiters that don't agree with this. They want to see what you're interested in to see if you're a cultural fit. I think it doesn't matter.

Diversity in the workplace means just that. Diversity. I don't need to know that you're a soccer fanatic because if I know the hiring manager and the rest of their team are huge soccer fans and play in an after work league, it can skew my opinion or those of the team.

I think of it a bit like the 'beer test'. There's an old school test that interviewers use. Would I have a beer with this candidate? If so, hire them!

I feel this way about hobbies, interests, and affiliations. Everyone has unconscious bias, and the goal of your resume and cover letter should be to display who you are as a professional. I think it's very admirable when people are involved in animal rescues and do volunteer work. Will that bias my opinion? Maybe? I try not to, but I love animals and if I equate your resume to my fluffy Malamute rescue, you might get past me and to the hiring manager. But what if I had a really bad experience with a specific organization that you name? I may hold that against you. And again, I'm not saying I would consciously make these decisions. Unconscious bias creeps in, and maybe there's something on your resume that wouldn't have bothered me before, but now I'm more likely to pass on you because I have a bias towards or against an organization you're affiliated with.

We absolutely want to know more about you as a person, but I'd rather learn about that in a conversation where there is some context rather than let something on a piece of paper deter someone. You don't know who will be on the other side of the resume so focus on your experience and technical skills.

Photos, Borders, Columns

There are a few reasons I want you to leave your photos off a resume.

First and foremost, not every ATS (applicant tracking system) accepts photos or heavily formatted resumes. When it comes to photos, I had a lot of resumes come through as an empty first page, a HUGE photo of someone's face that took up the whole screen, and then a resume several blank pages down. You can try submitting your resume as a PDF. I've seen those come through just fine, other times, not so much. Why risk a weird formatting situation that makes the recruiter hesitate?

Also, as mentioned before, from a diversity perspective we want to see your qualifications. Any time I had a resume come through with a photo on it, whether I was an internal or agency recruiter, I removed the picture before I sent it on to the hiring manager or anyone on the team. I wanted that candidate to be given a fair, unbiased opportunity to land the job, so I'd take the time to pull the photo off or block it out.

The borders, columns, graphics, etc. that people like to add, unless you are applying for a digital artwork role, graphic designer, or some other type of artistic or marketing role, leaving off the heavy formats and graphics are your best bet to get through an ATS. As a recruiter sometimes reviewing hundreds upon hundreds of resumes on a Monday morning, I'd find it jarring to click to the next resume only to find photos and emojis all around the border of each page. If I tried to download and send them as an attachment to a hiring manager, sometimes I'd be blocked, and sometimes the attachment would be too large. So the candidate would stand out, but not necessarily in a good way.

In some cases, I'd be able to decipher the candidate's experience well enough to want to screen them and then ask for their resume in a less formatted document. However, sometimes these resumes came through so convoluted that I had no idea what their experience was, and I didn't have time to follow up with them to get a different resume. This was different for me as an agency recruiter as I'd be more willing to work with a candidate because I had more time and could help format their resume. As an internal recruiter, not a chance. There's not enough time and I wasn't paid to help candidates. I was there to find the right talent for our organization and quickly.

You want to catch a recruiter's attention quickly and efficiently while not making it more difficult for them to share your information or resume with the hiring team.

Job Description Resumes

You want your resume to read about your accomplishments. Your outputs. What you were able to complete while employed at your past companies. Too often than not, resumes read like a list of job duties and responsibilities. Recruiters and hiring managers know what an accountant does. They know what an IT developer does. What they don't know, is what you accomplished. What did you complete while you worked for X company?

Companies want to know what you're capable of and what you bring to the table.

For Example:

- Wrote code for various IT applications used by other departments.

VS.

- Developed an IT application for the recruiting team that allowed recruiters to track sources of applications and measure time to fill. The talent attraction team was able to identify their top three sources of candidates and redirect spending of marketing efforts to save $200k over the course of 12 months. By measuring time to fill they were able to identify process improvements in the interview process and onboarding procedures that reduced time to fill from 68 days to 45 days.

Which one is going to stand out to you? Which one is going to leave a lasting impression and make you want to call them?

The one that saved the company time and money.

Here's what the bullet points should cover on your resume:

- **Problem:** What was the problem or issue you were trying to resolve? What details does the reader need to know to understand the situation fully?
- **Action:** What action did you take, or what were the tasks involved that led to the end solution?
- **Result:** What happened? What is the quantifiable outcome? (Think money, time, retention of people, positive reductions or increases, etc.)

You want the reader to review your resume and see that you can address an issue that they're trying to resolve. If they're posting a position, there is a problem that they are trying to solve. Each role has a purpose, and your ability to show yourself as the answer to their problems is what is going to win you that interview.

Resumes that read like a copy/paste of a job description get passed by. You may very well be capable of the role and all that it entails. You may be overqualified. But I won't know how the tasks that you have at X company correlate to what we're working on. Seeing what people have done and what they are capable of makes a lasting impression, and I'm more likely to remember that you implemented a new application or process that saved money and time versus managing meetings and participating in strategy discussions.

This is where customizing for the job that you're applying for comes in. If you listed every accomplishment you've ever had, you'd have a 10 page resume! Highlight the ones that you know are relevant based on the job description.

When I'm coaching clients, I have them come up with a list of all of their accomplishments. I help wordsmith them, and then they have a list of all of the great things they've done! More on this in a little bit!

Length of Resume

You've read what I just said about how to list your responsibilities, and you're now confused about how you're going to fit all of that on one piece of paper.

If you have more than three to five years of experience, you're not. Plain and simple.

Gone is the age old rule of one page resumes.

However, no seven page resumes, please.

For each role that you are applying to, you will need to find the skills and results that you've had that correlate to the job posting. Find three to five items for each role that you have, and list those on your resume. If you have some really great accomplishments that you want to share but can't seem to find a spot for them in the body of your resume, discuss them in a cover letter or add a small accomplishments section at the top of your resume.

When you get past 10 years, truncate that experience. One to two bullet points if necessary under those job headings. Two full pages for someone with consistent employment and 8-10 years or more of experience is acceptable. Three pages is starting to stretch it but can be justified for higher level leadership roles or uniquely technical roles.

If you have changed jobs every 12-18 months and you have 12 jobs to list for the last 10 years, prioritize the roles where you gained the most experience, and the roles that are relevant to the job. List every job in chronological order, but shorten what you share about roles that are irrelevant to the job you're applying for.

It seems like a lot of work to customize a resume for each job, but it's worth it in the long run. With a solid foundation, you can spend 10 minutes customizing your resume for each role rather than doing a complete rewrite every time a new job pops up on a job board.

I advise clients in my career services firm to give me their accomplishments for each role with quantifiable results. We spend time carving out what they've done, what they're proud of and what they feel the most comfortable talking about in an interview. I send them off with homework to take a day or two to think through each role they've had and what they are most proud of in each role.

Once we have the list, we prioritize and come up with a resume template for them. They have a core resume that will be applicable most of the time. Then they have a list of other accomplishments that didn't make the resume, but may be relevant to different employers, and they can plug and play as they need to. This gives the clients the opportunity to really think about what they've done and what they hope to do in their next role, but it also gives them the ability to demonstrate their best to a potential employer. (This is also great preparation for an interview!)

With a list of accomplishments ready to go, my clients can add/subtract whatever makes sense based on the job description for the role that they are applying for. This gives them quick customizations that take only a few minutes to complete when applying and ensures that their resume is an informative, comprehensive telling of their professional story.

Cover Letters

To use them or not to use them. That is the million dollar question.

My answer is going to frustrate you, sorry…

It depends on the situation.

Here's when I say you must use them:

- You are relocating and applying to jobs that you could not reasonably commute to, and they are not remote roles
- The company application requires it
- You are applying for a role outside of your industry or profession (making a career change)
- You are applying for leadership roles
- The job is a super stretch for you, but you're interested and up for the challenge
- There are large gaps or other odd events on your resume that you know an employer will be confused by or have questions about

That covers most scenarios, doesn't it? Maybe.

If the application or company doesn't have a spot for it or doesn't ask for it, don't include one. If you're doing a one click application through a job board or LinkedIn, you won't need to include one. You're being referred to the company by a friend or former colleague, you might not need one and can select the friend/referral name in the application. You've been recruited by an agency or corporate recruiter for the role, you probably won't need one.

My advice, use your best judgment. If you think you probably need one based on the application process, your situation, or the competitiveness of your role, then do it.

As a recruiter, I've never looked at a cover letter before someone's resume. I do, however, look for one if there is something that I have a question on in their resume. If I see that they are out of state or are in a different profession or industry, etc., I'll look to see if they've answered some of my questions in their cover letter.

Another thing I'd like to note is that while not having a cover letter has never hurt a candidate who I was reviewing, having one that was addressed to the wrong company or with a ton of errors in it, has hurt the candidate. If you're going to write a cover letter, be thoughtful and intentional about it, and make sure to have someone proofread it.

I have never sent a cover letter to the hiring manager. Never. All of those cover letters addressed to the hiring manager instead of me, they didn't see them. Hiring managers expect that the recruiter will vet out candidates before they review them. I've had a handful of managers who would try to review candidates before I did, but hiring isn't their main job, and they would start off with good intentions, but could rarely continue that level of involvement if the search went on for any length of time.

I didn't take it personally when the cover letters were addressed to the hiring manager, so address them to who you feel comfortable sending them to. It's more common that a recruiter is reviewing your resume and choosing who to screen and send to the hiring manager, so do some research on networking sites and make the best choice you can.

One Last Scenario

One last situation that comes up, that I didn't include in my list of when to use a cover letter, is an incredibly technical role.

I have recruited for difficult, technical engineering and IT roles my entire career. A few times I've had applicants write cover letters, addressed to me, that explained the technical aspects of their experience and how it related to the job description that I had posted. They did not reiterate their resume, and they didn't assume I didn't know what I was recruiting for. These applicants knew that their roles were highly technical and that their experience corresponded with the role that I was hiring for, but because they used different technologies or were in a different industry, I might not see the connection from a six second glance through their resume.

I appreciated these candidates connecting the dots in an incredibly professional way and using a cover letter to do so. It helped me learn the roles that I was recruiting for as well! Technical recruiters learn from the people who they recruit, and the candidates who took the time to explain a few of their projects and how they were similar to what we were doing helped me better understand their experience as well as what other areas related to the work we were doing. And, yes, I hired them.

Chapter 4: Best of the Worst Resume Stories

Are there really horror stories about resumes?

Yes. There sure are!

One of my favorite resumes was a resume with only two sentences on it:

1997- Present

Stock Clerk at The Only Retail Store in Town

That was it. Yes, it actually said, "the only retail store in town".

There were, in fact, about six retail stores in that town, and the resume also didn't have their name on it. They had put in a first and last name on the application but didn't fill out the contact information. This candidate angrily called into our main office a few weeks later when they hadn't been contacted for an interview. The call had been routed to me since I was the recruiter assigned to the position, and when I told this candidate that they hadn't filled out the application entirely and that their resume didn't have any identifying information on it, they argued with me.

I explained to the candidate that the position was actually for an accounting role and that they didn't have the necessary experience required for the role. They told me that they had been an accountant for over 10 years. I was staring at the resume, explaining that I didn't see that and that information wasn't on their resume. It took us 10 minutes to reach the conclusion that they hadn't filled out the application completely before hitting the submit button.

The candidate sent me a copy of their resume via email, but we had already completed the final round of interviews and were making an offer the next day. This candidate did come around and apologize and was embarrassed once they realized what happened, but had they not called in, they would have never known that they didn't complete the application or upload an actual resume.

I have no idea how this person had a resume that just listed an old high school job. I still don't know which retail store they worked at.

The Runner Up Resume....

My runner up for favorite resume was a resume that was 17 pages long. Yes. Seventeen pages. It was just pictures too. No words except for the end where they put their contact information (at least we had contact information this time!).

The border of each page was the same – family photos, vacation photos, the Muppets, bands, and tv show characters. The body of the resume contained photos of company logos followed by pictures of the candidate with their coworkers.

How this resume came through our ATS is beyond me. It shouldn't have been able to get through since the file was massive. It's obvious that the candidate was trying to grab our attention. It worked. But not in the way that they wanted. We didn't know the types of roles that they had been in, what they had done, or what their career progression was like.

I knew where the candidate had vacationed, what shows and bands they liked, and other personal interests that I could determine from the pictures on the border of the resume, but I had zero idea what their background was or how it correlated to the work that we were doing. This candidate didn't make it through to a screen, and they could have been qualified, but there wasn't a recruiter on my team that had the time to dig in and find out.

One of the more common occurrences when candidates are applying for roles is that they apply using documents other than their resumes. Some of the things that I have seen uploaded instead of a resume:

- Utility Bills
- Tax Returns
- Insurance Papers
- Gym Contracts
- Receipts
- Expense Reports
- Spouse's Resume
- Blank Resume Templates
- Work Presentations
- Confidential Company Documents
- Medical Test Results

The best advice I can give anyone for making sure this doesn't happen to them is to save your resume in a very clear format. For example, my resume is saved as:

Jaime Schmitt Resume

If by some chance you do upload something other than what you should have, many applicant tracking systems have a candidate portal where you can login and change the documents you uploaded. If you can't do that, there's nothing wrong with emailing the recruiting team with your resume and explaining that you made a mistake. I've had plenty of people email me copies of their resume, telling me that they accidentally sent an outdated one, or they thought it might not have gone through the system correctly (or that they sent me their utility bill!), and I've never held it against them.

Truth be told, these situations happened most often when I was an internal recruiter. As an agency recruiter, I was reaching out to candidates and they were sending me word documents of their resumes. Occasionally, I'd receive an outdated resume, but that was few and far between. You don't want internal recruiters to get the wrong documents because as we've discussed before, they don't have the time or incentive to follow up with you to get the right documents. So if you notice your error, and really want the job, try to correct the course. However, don't expect a company's recruiter to reach out to you to let you know that they now have a copy of your medical test results!

You absolutely want to lead with your best foot forward, but sometimes mistakes happen. Brush it off, do your best to correct it, and if the company declines you because of it, use it as a learning lesson, and find the next great opportunity!

Chapter 5: Networking, Making Friends in the Job Search Game

I've had people tell me that they've never had to network to find a new job until recently. I've had others tell me that every job they've ever found for the last 30+ years has been through networking and referrals. From my experience, networking has become more prevalent in the last several years so while some people have been referred to every job they've had, there are a lot of people who are learning to network for the first time.

If you're out searching for a new position, my recommendation is always to network to your level of comfort. If you are miserably uncomfortable going to speed networking events or other local in person networking events, maybe don't attend an event as your first attempt at networking. If you don't use social media well and would rather have a root canal over posting on social media, then try an event. If you are uncomfortable with a mode of networking, it's going to show, so start with what makes you most comfortable.

There are multiple ways you can network for a new role. Here are a few ways to approach the networking game:

- *Join virtual groups on LinkedIn, Facebook, Stack Overflow, etc.* There are groups that you can join where jobs are posted, career advice is shared, etc. These are great ways to network, and I recommend everyone do this regardless of whether they're job searching or not.

- ***Local/national chapters of organizations specific to your industry.*** I'll use SHRM for example (as I'm in the HR field). They have local and national chapters. You can join their organization and get access to virtual and local events, network with other people in your field, learn about new things going on in your industry to keep your knowledge up to date. These are great resources for more than just networking.
- ***Conferences, seminars, classes.*** Local universities, trade schools, and organizations often host continuing education classes or workshops that are great for meeting new people in your area and industry. Conferences are also a fantastic way to network within your profession as well as learn new skills and enhance your current skill set.

These are great ways to meet people and share that you're looking for new roles, but what about right now? You're applying for a position now, and you want to make a connection with someone at the company, what do you do?

I coach all of my clients to research the company and their employees on LinkedIn. When you're looking for a job, look up the company on LinkedIn. Who do you know that works there? If they're someone you actually know and have met, send them a message sharing your interest and that you've applied. OR, see if they're open to sharing what they like about the company and their role if you're on the fence about the company.

Someone you just happen to be connected to, but don't know them personally?

Introduce yourself and explain that you're interested in the company and wanted to see what their experience was like. They will probably tell you, AND they will probably tell their recruiter that someone reached out to them about X role.

In every company I've worked for, people that I didn't know at the company would reach out to me to tell me that someone reached out to them to ask about a role that I was recruiting for. They would send me their name, their resume, if it had been sent, and a summary of the correspondence. This happened to me several times a week throughout my entire career. You can network without asking for a referral, and you may still get a referral!

What about reaching out to the hiring manager or recruiter directly?

People message me directly for jobs that I have posted all the time. All. The. Time. If you do some searching, you'll see mixed feedback and feelings about this from recruiters.

Do I mind when people reach out to me directly and ask me to review their resume? Not at all.

Do I mind when people reach out asking me when I'm available to interview them? I don't care for this approach very much, and I'll tell you why.

As a recruiter, I very much want to fill a position and take the burden off my hiring manager and their team. However, I want to be fair to all candidates and follow our process. I understand people want to jump ahead of the competition. I think a well worded message that shares your interest and lets me know that you've applied is great. It does what the person is trying to accomplish.

However, asking for an interview on a social media platform, outside of the recruiting process that the company has established, puts me in an awkward position. Recruiters are moving at a hundred miles an hour juggling so many things in the air. While I use LinkedIn for business, it's still owned by me as a personal profile. It's not part of the company's tools and hiring process. I shouldn't be discussing an interview process with you on social media. That should go through my company email or phone communication. Companies get audited on their recruiting process. It has happened to me that I didn't have emails that I should have during an audit. The messages were in my LinkedIn messenger. I didn't pass that section of my audit, and it was absolutely on me. I couldn't move those messages to company email so I wouldn't have passed that section of my audit unless I had restarted the same conversation with the candidate via email. No one has time to do that.

I review every resume that I receive. I always have. A thoughtful, well written message on LinkedIn expressing your interest in the role and company is great and will get people's attention. Even if we don't respond to your message (we just can't sometimes, there are hundreds), we read it, and it sticks with us. Just like I read every resume that passes my desk, I read every LinkedIn message I get.

I do encourage all of my career services clients to reach out to the recruiters or connections that they have on LinkedIn. However, I coach them on a few things:

- Make sure you are really qualified for the role.
    - If you are a two-year experienced application developer, and you are applying for a senior developer role that requires 10 years minimum experience, we shouldn't be applying to that position. Quite often when people reach out to me for a role that they applied to, they are an IT Application Developer applying to a Supply Chain Manager role (or some other combination of roles that they are really not qualified for).
- Keep it short, simple and to the point.
    - Messages that are three plus pages long just aren't going to be read. Your

message doesn't need to be the length of a tweet, but it can't be a novel either. Shorter than a cover letter is all you need to share that you're interested in the role and why.

- Be professional and sincere.
    - Think of it as another chance to express your interest. A canned message that gets sent to every recruiter doesn't show interest, and we can tell when you've sent it to every other company you've applied to. Reach out when this is a role, company, manager that you really want to work for. That level of interest speaks volumes.

Something you do not want to do when reaching out to the hiring team directly is be rude, make assumptions, or insist that you be interviewed. I'll share more later about some not-so-great encounters I've had in regards to networking as these interactions hold a lasting impression. There are people who are one of a few in their industry or profession that I wouldn't call if they were the last person on the earth that could do the job, and it's because of how they treated one of the members on the hiring team.

Referrals, Referrals, Referrals!

Companies have referral policies in place because they know one of their greatest sources of candidates comes from their own employees referring their friends, family, and professional network. As an internal recruiter, I received referrals regularly, and when we were having trouble with difficult positions, we would increase the referral bonuses we were paying.

You've networked and reached out and you're being referred into a company! Great! So do you still have to go through the regular recruiting process?!

Yes, you should, and you should expect that. Referrals absolutely have a way of going around a standard recruitment process, but they shouldn't, and you shouldn't, expect to skirt the process because you were referred into a company. Think about it from this perspective, if you weren't referred in, you would want all candidates to be treated the same so that everyone had the same opportunity for the role.

What does a referral earn you?

Getting your resume reviewed and potentially a call with the recruiter for the role.

I spoke to every referral I was given when I was an internal recruiter. Even if a candidate wasn't qualified, I would spend a few minutes on the phone with them and consider them for other roles in the future. I did that because of my relationship with my internal employees that referred the candidates.

A referral didn't earn them an interview with the hiring manager and didn't earn them a job offer.

Referrals were oftentimes great fits for the roles that I was hiring for. Where things would go south is that these candidates didn't interview the greatest because they thought the job was theirs. You still have to go through the process, and you still have to interview. As a recruiter, I would love when I would get a referral because our internal employees know the company and they know what we look for. They've already vetted the candidate and are recommending them with their reputation at stake. When a referral candidate came across entitled or unprofessional, it was disappointing for everyone involved.

It might sound like I don't like referral candidates, and I can assure you that is not the case. I loved getting referrals and I've hired hundreds of referrals over the years. I have just often seen referrals not get a job offer because of how they handled their communications, the interview process, and their lack of self-awareness throughout. When you're referred to a company, thank the referrer, and go through the process like the rest of the candidates. You have a leg up because you are a known and recommended candidate, but humbleness goes a long way with hiring teams!

Do I Have to Network?

No, but yes.

It is 100% possible that you will apply to a position, not be referred, know absolutely no one at the company, not reach out to the hiring team and still get the job. It happens every day.

But it's easier to find your next great role or your dream job if you network and meet people.

When you network you not only gain connections with people you meet but the people that those people know as well.

For example: I meet Katie at a conference. We exchange information and backgrounds and go back to our lives, but Katie now knows that I'm in the market for a new job. A few weeks later, her friend Andrea, posts on social media asking her network if they know anyone that is in the market for a new recruiting job. Katie knows that I'm looking, remembers me and tags me in the post. Now, Andrea has found a potential candidate and I've found a potential job that neither of us would have run across if Katie wouldn't have known us both.

It's the seven degrees of separation! Everyone can be connected to the right opportunity or person, but you have to meet people and build relationships. Finding your next role is about being in the right place at the right time with the right people.

Chapter 6: Networking in Action

Referrals and networking can change the trajectory of your career, and it can make opportunities appear when you're not expecting it. Every job that I ever had, I was referred in. Those referrals didn't get me the job, and I was qualified for all of the positions that I applied for, but it gave me professional credibility and a foot in the door.

Other than a first job while I was in high school where I just applied at the store's kiosk, did a quick onsite interview five minutes later and left my shopping trip with a new job, (this never happens anymore and it's a bit surreal even thinking about this!), I've been referred to a company or had a past coworker that worked at the new company I was applying to who referred me in. Even now as a consultant, my gigs come from word of mouth and referrals.

Keeping in touch with former coworkers or colleagues, even through social media like LinkedIn, will help when you start looking for new roles.

When I'm coaching my clients, one of the first things I ask them is: Who do you know? When you're applying to a role, who do you know that could give you a referral? This has opened so many doors for some of my clients, and one thing I always tell them is to be patient. Maybe it's not your dream job now, but maybe it's something down the road.

Sometimes people will do the networking for you. As a recruiter, I have other recruiter friends. When I can't hire someone or don't have anything for them, but I know they're marketable, I send them to my recruiter friends. I did this a ton as an internal candidate. People would apply and not be right for a role or be out of the salary range, but my recruiter friends had similar roles. I'd pass them along.

I had a position that I had been working on forever. Forever. It hadn't had its one-year birthday, but it was close. It was a very niche role, and we wanted the world for a standard salary. One day a resume hit my resume, and it was the absolute perfect fit. This resume had been passed to me by another internal recruiter at another company. She didn't have anything for this candidate, but their spouse had taken a role with her company and this was the trailing spouse who was looking. The spouse that had a new role with this company passed their spouse's resume to the recruiter who hired them and asked if there was anything they could do.

She immediately looked at other roles in the area and saw that I was hiring for a role that would fit the spouse's background. I would have never found this candidate, at least not easily, as they weren't located in the geographic areas that we were looking in. I didn't know this candidate was relocating. I wouldn't have run into them.

By the new hire networking and sharing their spouse's resume, and my recruiter colleague networking, we both filled hard to fill positions and both spouses found new jobs. I'm sure the first spouse felt awkward sending their spouse's resume onto the recruiter at their new company, but we were all glad that they did!

Years ago, I was at a campus recruiting event, and someone from another company who was working their booth, came up to me and said, "I have a cousin that applied for your company. It was for your XYZ role. Would you be willing to look at their resume?"

Yes, I sure would!

The person had been chatting with their cousin via text, and the cousin had said "If this company is there, can you ask them to look at my resume?"

I was able to pull up the resume, review it, ping my recruiter colleague and ask them to contact the candidate for an interview. The candidate had multiple offers and ended up not taking ours (we would have been a longer daily commute at the time), but they had an opportunity because someone was willing to ask a question on their behalf.

Here's yet another example of how things can work out with networking.

Someone who I had worked with professionally, (they were a vendor that our company worked with), added me on LinkedIn. A few months later they shared a post of a former colleague who had been downsized at their previous company. I saw the post, contacted them and asked them to put me directly in touch with the former colleague who had been downsized. Match made.

Still not convinced you need to network?

One more example.

A manager, for a company that I worked for, lived in a different country. They received a resume from a former colleague who had received the resume from their brother. Follow that? This manager sent the resume to me for a position that I had in another country than the one he lived in. His former colleague's brother (and the person whose resume it was) lived in the United States, but this resume took a trip through European email to get redirected back to me.

Yes, I hired the referral from the manager that came from his former colleague's brother. Another great match.

It's incredibly intimidating to network. As someone who does it professionally for a living, I still get nervous meeting new people or asking for a referral. Always. It's an incredibly vulnerable position to find yourself in, especially if you have been downsized and are anxiously trying to find a new role. But it has the power to move mountains for you, and referrals can spiral to levels that you never imagined.

I cannot count how many times a referral has gotten to me, and the referred person doesn't even know who the person is who ultimately gave me the resume because their resume has been passed down the line to the next person and to the next person.

So go out there and make some friends! It will be worth it!

Chapter 7: Interviewing 101

We've all had to interview at some point in our careers and anyone who feels a hundred percent confident interviewing is either lying, or maybe they've just interviewed too many times! Changing jobs is stressful. Interviewing is even more stressful. You're being judged on a snapshot of time and based on only a few questions.

As someone who has interviewed others for quite a while, I still get nervous in the event I have to interview for something, and I have never had a situation where I was asked something I wasn't prepared for! My best advice to anyone in the job search is to set yourself up for success and study like you were studying for an exam!

Here are some of my top must do's for any interview:

1. Know the position that you applied for.
2. Be prepared.
3. Dress appropriately for the role and the company.
4. Follow up after the interview.

Let's dive a bit deeper into each of these areas.

Know the Position You've Applied For

What do I mean by this?

I mean that you actually have to remember which role you've applied for when a recruiter or hiring manager contacts you. Too many times I've had people tell me they don't even remember applying for the role, or they don't know which role I've applied for because they've applied for so many. That may be true, but try not to find yourself in that situation.

For every role that you've applied for, track it. In a spreadsheet. In a notebook. Wherever it makes sense to you to track it. Keep track of the role, the company, the date you applied, and the job description. Most companies keep roles posted until they are filled, but why make more work for yourself by having to go and find the job description on their website? When I've applied in the past, I've downloaded a copy of the job description or copy and pasted it into a word document so that I had it.

Create digital folders with the resume, cover letter, and job description along with your tracker, or print stuff out and have paper folders. I don't care what your method is, but track it.

As a recruiter, nothing turned me off of a candidate faster than them telling me either 1) they didn't know what jobs they had applied for and/or 2) the candidate asked me to send them the job description. Recruiters are looking for people who want to work for the company and who are excited about it. If you tell them you're applying to so many jobs you can't remember what you applied to, and you need to see the job description, you're missing the mark.

Most interview requests are going to come through your email. Do your homework and if you truly can't find the job application you submitted or the job description posted, then ask the interviewer/recruiter if the job is posted somewhere as you would like to review it again prior to an interview.

Once you get to the interview make sure that you have reviewed the job description prior to the interview as this leads to our next step.

Be Prepared

Research the company. Review the job description. Come prepared with questions. Practice for standard interview questions.

When preparing for an interview I tell my candidates that they need to prepare for an interview like they would for a test. Review the information available to you, and come prepared for what you think will be on the exam.

The candidates that did the best in interviews with me showed that they had done their homework on the company. They were able to tell me things about the company that weren't on the first page of the website. Candidates who shared what we were doing from a community perspective, or had dug into what the company was doing from a business development perspective, caught my attention. I was always impressed when candidates were able to tell me about an article that they had read about a project or product we were working on, or they were able to tell me about how they would be able to impact a certain initiative the company was working on. That helped me sell them to the hiring manager and give them the "what was in it for them" when it came to hiring the candidate.

Next, I tell my candidates to review the job description and make sure you understand the general overview of expectations for the role. If there is something that doesn't make sense or isn't clear, write it down. You need a list of questions to ask the interviewer so start your list here.

With the job description in front of you, you can start to make a list of areas that you know the interviewer will question you about. The list of technical requirements will be an area of focus during the interview so make sure you have examples and can speak to your ability in these areas.

There will most likely be a mix of traditional interview questions (ex: Tell me about yourself) and behavioral questions (Tell me about a time when you…) so be prepared to answer both. We'll get to this a bit later.

Dress Appropriately

With today's virtual, hybrid, more casual environments it can be difficult to know what the appropriate attire is for an interview. How do we plan? Do we overdress? What happens if we underdress?

I coach my candidates to ask the recruiter if they don't tell you. It is completely ok to ask an internal recruiter at a company what the preferred attire is for interviews. If you're interviewing at a manufacturing company, it is completely possible they may want you to tour the floor. Having certain footwear may be required for this (I'll give you a personal story on this in the next chapter!). Or maybe there will be important clients onsite the day of your interview, so they will want everyone in professional attire, and you'll want to blend in.

There's nothing more uncomfortable than being the only person in extremely professional attire, or completely underdressed, for an interview.

No guidance from the recruiter?

My advice is then to err on the side of overdressing rather than underdressing. You don't want to be the one in jeans when everyone else is in a suit.

Most environments are now more business casual and dressing for their days (dressing up for external meetings, and dressing more casual for a day of internal meetings), but it won't hurt you to ask and seek guidance.

For a virtual interview, I recommend still asking if you're unsure. I also recommend sticking with your attire for top and bottom. I have a funny story I'll share in the stories chapter, but from a confidence perspective, I believe you will feel more confident and put together if you're dressed professionally from top to bottom.

Follow Ups

Do you still need to follow up with a thank you note after an interview?

Yes.

I regularly receive requests for hiring managers', hiring teams', and HRs' email addresses after an interview so that the candidate could send a follow up email thanking them for their time and consideration. Hiring teams still look for this and still evaluate candidates on this.

The best time to send off a thank you email is shortly after your interview. This way the interview is still fresh in their minds, and you're cementing yourself in their memory. If you wait a few days, and there have been a few interviews in between your interview and your communication, they may wonder what took you so long or they may have forgotten details of your interview.

You want to send a note later that day, or early the next day, thanking them and sharing that you're interested in next steps. This gives the interviewer a sense of urgency. You are in their inbox and looking for a response or next steps. They will be more likely to move you along or give you an answer than if you wait a week. If you don't have urgency, they won't either.

Want bonus points? Email the recruiter after a phone screen interview and then again if you've made it to the team interview portion. When I received thank you emails I was always a little taken aback. Recruiters don't get thanked very often and certainly not for phone screens. We usually don't get thanked for pushing candidates through to an interview process and supporting them throughout either.

I've had numerous situations where a team was between two candidates and hiring managers would ask if I received thank you emails or what my communication had been like with the candidates. The candidate who sent me thank you notes and was easier for me to work with got the job offer… every single time.

Why?

Because the hiring managers liked seeing candidates that could work with other teams, had a high level of customer service, and were professional and polite.

Candidates who were rude to me or didn't want to work with me and would jump over me to get to the hiring manager? The managers saw right through that, and those candidates were penalized.

Thank your recruiter, and be polite and professional, and your recruiter will go to battle for you.

Types of Interviews: Traditional vs. Behavioral Questions

Most interviews are going to be a blend of interview styles. It's only natural for interviewers to have some general questions to learn more about your background and then behavioral questions to assess your ability to problem solve, think strategically, and work with teams.

You can set yourself up for success when you write your resume to be more accomplishments focused versus task oriented as we discussed earlier. As an interviewer, I would prepare questions based on what someone had on their resume and then a few other questions to flush out information that they maybe didn't include on their resume. This is where it becomes important to make sure you are very familiar with your own resume, and you're prepared to answer questions in the STAR format (we'll cover this shortly).

With traditional questions, be prepared for open ended questions like:

- Tell me about yourself.
- Why did you get into IT?
- What are your strengths and weaknesses?
- What would your coworkers say about you? Your manager?
- What do you like least about your job? What do you like the most?
- Why do you want to work here?
- What questions do you have?
- What are your career goals?

The list goes on, but you get the idea. Be prepared to talk about YOU! Your hopes, dreams, desires, likes, and dislikes. This is all fair game for an interview to ask.

You should not be asked any questions that relate to your:

- Race
- Ethnicity
- Gender
- Religion
- Age
- Marital Status

What happens if an interviewer asks you a question that you know they legally shouldn't be asking?

I'd love to tell you that in 2023 this kind of stuff doesn't happen anymore, but I'd be lying to you.

Interviewers still ask way more inappropriate questions than they should. It happens.

You are well within your rights to say that you don't feel comfortable answering that question. However, I know most candidates will just answer the question for fear of being viewed as difficult or not compliant.

Answer to your comfort level, or tell the interviewer that you'd feel more comfortable answering questions that assessed your ability to do the responsibilities of the job.

The two most common ways I've seen these protected areas violated are with questions like this:

- When do you plan on retiring? How much longer do you plan on working?
- Do you have a family? Do you plan on having a family?

Again, answer to your comfort level or redirect the conversation. Will it hurt your chances of getting the job? Maybe. But do you want to work for a company or manager who thinks it's appropriate to ask those questions?

STAR Method

There are other acronyms, but the one that I like the best (because it's easy for me to remember and stars and unicorns go well together) is the STAR behavioral interviewing method.

STAR stands for:

S- Situation

T- Task

A- Action

R- Result

In behavioral based interviewing, interviewers are looking for examples of past performance and behaviors that will give them an idea of what your future performance and behaviors will be like if they were to hire you.

Here is an example of a STAR answer for a Business Analyst working with a recruiting team for system improvements.

Situation - You need to give enough information that the interviewer understands what was going on, but they don't need to know that Suzy, from accounting, and Bill, from supply chain, and Gina, from HR, all did XYZ.

The situation should be the shortened version of the situation and not the in depth version you give to your boss when you're briefing them on the story.

It could look something like this:

The problem came from the head of recruitment and HR. It was taking them 14 clicks to post a job and about 30 minutes to get that job live. When reviewing applications, the resume and applications were on separate pages, and it took recruiters about 3 minutes per application to pull up a candidate account and review it. Recruiters were backlogged and felt that the administrative tasks were taking too long based on system limitations.

The interviewer has the layout. You haven't divulged confidential information, and you haven't shared names. They have the 100ft view of the situation.

Task - Here you need to give them what the objective and task is. We know from the situation that there's an issue, but what actually has to be done? This is the tactical piece of the situation.

Your task could be as simple as this:

My team was tasked with improving our system's performance by decreasing the amount of time it took for recruiters to process applications and post jobs. We knew from the head of recruitment that the system was slow with a lot of clicks and layout issues. My task was to document the data, and to observe and duplicate the issues the recruiting team was experiencing.

Simple. You need information to take action. That was your task, and you kept it simple.

Action - Here's where you share what you did. What other actions were required. What happened to resolve the situation?

I documented the data by sitting with the recruiters and watching them post jobs and review candidates. I collected the times and ruled out human error. I then replicated the issues that they were experiencing.

I determined that there were multiple steps in the posting process that weren't needed by the recruiting team so we removed those steps and simplified the process. The lag time in reviewing applications is a known system issue so we engaged the vendor to rectify this situation. The layout of the resumes/applications was a simple customization issue, and we resolved this by changing the layout to one that streamlined the application review process for the recruiters.

I gathered the requirements, collected data, and then worked with our HRIS and IT team to develop the solutions. IT, HRIS and I relayed the enhancements back to the recruiting team and worked with them on testing and implementing the process forward. I, with the help of IT, created the change documents.

Done. They know what you did and who you collaborated with. Great!

Result - The R in STAR is RESULTS!! What's in it for them? Here is where you need tangible data. Data and results that the interviewer can hold.

Based on our current example. What was the end result of these job posting and application review processes?

After implementing these system improvements, our job posting process was down to 7 clicks or steps, and it was only taking recruiters 10 minutes to complete a job posting! That cut down the process system clicks by 50% and it was a 66% reduction in time per job posting for the recruiters! Applications and resumes were on the same page now, and recruiters could review each resume and application in under 10 seconds versus 3 minutes for the toggling and load times!

What did the interviewer just learn about you?

You can handle a problem. You engaged the stakeholders and collaborated with other teams. You can expedite a cumbersome process. You can save them time and money.

Think they'll have follow up questions and want to ask you more about your process such as how you approached conversations and how you handled setbacks?

Absolutely they will. And you'll be ready!

Interviewing Gone Wrong

There are some things that can go terribly wrong during an interview. Here are some things that can happen that will ensure you're not getting a call back:

- Being unprepared
- Dressing inappropriately
- Talking excessively/tangents/irrelevant answers
- Criticizing previous employers/colleagues
- Unprofessional behavior
- Not asking questions

Being Unprepared

I talked a great deal about being prepared so it goes without saying that not being prepared is going to be a big red flag, but this goes beyond just not knowing a few pieces of information about the company.

This includes not showing up for the interview or confusing the times. Being late for an interview. Not knowing who the interviewers are. Flat out telling the interviewers you aren't prepared or that you didn't want to interview at this time/date but couldn't change it.

For a virtual interview, having people or animals running around screaming and squealing. or taking interviews in a car is distracting. Although, I have had people tell me they could interview at a certain time that was convenient for me but warned me they would be in their parked car. I appreciated them being willing to do that at noon on Tuesday versus asking me to interview them at 6 p.m. on a Friday. If you do have to do a virtual interview in a car, give the interviewer a heads up.

Bring something to write with and copies of your resume. Show that you're interested in the role, and it will go a long way.

Dressing Inappropriately

I'm not necessarily talking about under or overdressing here. I'm talking about shorts, flip flops (unless that's the culture, and you're told it's ok), and shirts that you're falling out of.

I once interviewed someone who had so much cat hair on them that I thought it was a different color suit. I have two huskies. I understand pet hair. But I shouldn't have to guess if your suit is black or gray because of clumps of cat hair falling off of you.

Ask what the dress code is and dress appropriately. If you dress in super business professional dress, but part of the interview is a tour through the manufacturing facility, you're going to be uncomfortable. This happened to me, and I clomped my way around a huge shop floor in stilettos. I do not recommend doing that.

Talking Excessively/Tangents/Irrelevant Information

I'm going to start with irrelevant information. Review job descriptions and ask the interviewer what the key aspects or requirements are for the role. Answer and provide information that is relative to those areas.

For example, I've worked for companies that did aerospace or government work and candidates who had security clearances would routinely apply because there was industry crossover. I have had candidates tell me repeatedly that they had a top secret security clearance. That is great for them, and there are companies that would love that. We didn't need it anywhere in our organization. That candidate was very proud of their clearance. As they should be. But the company wouldn't be able to maintain it for them, and they'd lose it. I knew that they would lose something that was really important to them.

Hiring managers weren't interested in hiring someone only to lose them shortly down the road when we couldn't provide them the type of work that would keep their certifications and clearances active. Maybe the candidate would have self selected out at some point during the interview process, but the hiring manager wasn't interested in continuing the candidacy because they ultimately couldn't meet what that candidate was looking for.

This has happened to me with other candidates and other qualifications. If you talk repeatedly about how much you enjoy reporting and talk about all of the reports that you create, manage, maintain, etc., and the job includes zero reporting, the interviewer is going to pass on you. They are looking for someone who wants to do the responsibilities that the role is asking for.

Where candidates have dropped out for me is when they talk excessively about their background or experience and don't allow enough time for the interviewer to ask questions. When I interview candidates, one of the first questions I ask them is, can you walk me through your background and fill me in a bit on you.

It's an open-ended question, and all I'm looking for is a high level overview of the candidate's education, work history, and why we're chatting. I'll ask further questions after that, but your background question answers should take no longer than a few minutes. When I'd book a 30-minute phone screen with a candidate, ask that question, and they would talk for 45 minutes after that question without coming up for air, it was an automatic decline.

The same goes for answers to any of the questions you've been asked. A few minutes answer, max, for a behavioral question, and then the interviewer will interject questions. An interview should be a conversation with back and forth dialog. If you find that you are talking a ton (it happens, people get nervous), try to give more clear and concise answers.

This takes us to tangents. It's happened to all of us where we were answering a question and forgot exactly where we were going with it or what was asked of us. It happens. But you can level set yourself, ask for clarification, stop and restart, etc. There are many ways to handle those situations. Where candidates go wrong is that they don't acknowledge it, and they continue in their convoluted answer. Then they sit back when they're done and either 1) don't know that they didn't give a coherent answer or 2) hope that the interviewer didn't catch on.

I once had a candidate give me an answer to a question that took multiple turns and twists, and I was so confused by the end that when he asked if I needed clarification on something all I could do was say, "Nope, guess you answered my question."

Because I couldn't even dissect what he had said to me.

There were stories about the candidate's kids, vacations, a coworker had an illness and was out on leave, and they had done a fundraiser for them, his manager had quit, and he was under a different team.

I have no idea what work related activities he did during all of this. Zero. No clue.

You don't want to be leaving the interviewer with a story or situation so confusing that they remember details like the ones I remember above. You want them to remember what you did in a situation. How you handled yourself and what was the outcome.

Talking Poorly About Past Coworkers and Employers

This is a tough one because people are going to ask why you're leaving a company. That question is going to come from a recruiter, interviewing team members, HR, and hiring managers. You're going to get asked this several times, and if you're leaving because of a poor culture or a bad manager, it can be hard to hide that if you're applying for a role that is a lateral move or even a step down from your current role. It can be difficult to hide that even if the role is a step up and your dream job!

I've interviewed so many people throughout my career that I can usually spot a cultural or managerial conflict for people when I ask, "Why are you looking for a new job?" They're vague, and they brush past it quickly. They will say they're just looking for career growth and opportunity for advancement but without a ton of substance as to why they can't find that at their current role.

This is the standard answer to this timeless question, but what about when you have a recruiter like me or interviewer who pushes further?

I like to ask:

Are there any opportunities for advancement at your current company?

One of the best responses I've received when I've asked this question was:

'There very well may be opportunities for advancement in the future, but at this time I'm pursuing opportunities outside of the company as I believe this gives me the best opportunity for personal growth and fulfillment that I'm seeking immediately.'

I understood. They wanted a new challenge. They wanted it now, and they had doubts about their current company. They didn't need to tell me that their company doesn't like to promote from within, or their manager is afraid to lose people so they won't promote.

As a third party agency recruiter, I've had people flat out tell me, "I can't get along with my manager. Four other people have left my team because of them and now I'm overworked, and we can't hire anyone, and I need out."

I appreciated the honesty, coached them on how to share why they were looking for a new job in an interview, and we moved on. This is how I coach my clients. You are moving onto something else. Something bigger and better. So why is the new company the golden ticket? What do they have to offer you that would enhance your career? That's why you're looking and interviewing. Use this information when you formulate your answer, and explain why you're leaving your current company. If there are negative feelings and undesirable situations at your current company, leave it there.

And what if you were terminated??

If you were restructured, this happens and the people you're interviewing with have probably heard about the layoffs at XYZ company. You can explain that you were part of a restructuring and are now seeking new employment. It's best to answer the question directly and leave emotion out of it. We all know being laid off is an emotional situation, but we're moving on! Look at the positives and share that with the interviewer just like we discussed above.

Example: *I was impacted by the most recent restructuring and downsizing initiatives at XYZ company, but this has given me a chance to explore new opportunities that will allow me to grow professionally.*

People get nervous answering this question, and I know I ramble when I'm nervous. I've interviewed enough nervous people to know that they all ramble when they're nervous too! Practice what you're going to say and be comfortable with it. Short, simple, and direct. Never say more words than you have to!

But what if you were termed for something you did? Or something you didn't do?

Mistakes happen and people get fired for it. Unless you made an egregious error and were terminated on the spot, usually there is a Performance Improvement Plan in place, or some type of corrective action in play, when people are terminated. Usually, not always. Regardless of how you were terminated, it's not a good idea to lie about it to cover it up. The odds are slim that this information will come back on a reference or background check, but you never know. It may.

I recommend avoiding words like *fired* or *terminated* and recommend using *let go* or *we mutually agreed that this wasn't the right fit for either of us.* It's a break up and whether you feel it was justified or not, it's best to be as professional about it as possible.

Unprofessional Behavior

As much as you're being evaluated on your answer to their questions, interviewers are assessing your behaviors as well. As an interviewer, I do look for guarded behavior or signs that might demonstrate you're being dishonest. However, I look for how you treat others more than anything else.

When I worked in a corporation and had a recruiting coordinator that would schedule interviews and often meet candidates in the lobby and take them to an interview room, I would ask my coordinator about the candidate's behaviors. I wanted to know if they were responsive, professional, polite, etc. I wanted to know how they treated the front desk person. In turn, hiring managers would often ask me how the candidate treated me as well. We were all looking for consistent, professional behaviors.

I had the absolute best recruiting coordinator who didn't want to say a bad word about anyone, but when I'd ask how they were treated, if it wasn't professional, the recruiting coordinator would say, "Maybe they're just stressed about the interview," or "I think we might have other candidates that would be a better cultural fit." You don't want to leave that type of impression with anyone if you're interviewing for a new role.

Being rude, short, or difficult with the people who are looking to hire you isn't going to make you friends. The interview isn't just the time that you're onsite or on camera interviewing, it's the whole process.

Not Asking Questions

Throughout the interview and towards the end, interviewers will give you time to ask questions. I've had some really great questions from candidates, some not so great questions, and some that had zero questions.

What happens if you've had all of your questions answered throughout the course of the interview?

Summarize your questions for the interviewer. Tell them the list of questions that you had prior to the interview (because you should have them on hand, written down), and summarize what you heard from the interviewer. This gives a chance for them to clarify anything, provide more information, and shows you were invested in the interview.

If you still have questions at the end of the interview, this is a great time to clarify any of the responsibilities, team functions and operations, and managerial expectations that you may have. Ask what projects you're going to be working on, and what you could do to prepare yourself for the job if you were to get an offer. Get a great understanding of what will be expected of you.

However, if your only question is about the salary and working hours, the interviewers aren't going to be impressed. Also, know your audience. There were so many candidates that I had in corporate who would ask their peers about salary. They had no idea. They knew what they made, but they couldn't answer what the role was paying. It wasn't the right audience. It's ok to clarify salary and working hours, most managers will answer this without being asked, but it should not be the only question you have.

To Summarize...

I could write an entire book on interviewing. There's a lot that can go wrong, but also a lot can go very right with preparation and practice.

If you remember anything from this chapter, I want you to remember this:

- Know the company
- Know the job

If you do your homework before the interview, the rest will follow and unless you show up in a Halloween costume or cuss out one of the interviewers, you're probably going to be just fine. It might not be the perfect match, but you're not going to leave feeling deflated or embarrassed. Interview to the best of your ability, and the rest is really out of your control.

Chapter 8: The Good, the Bad, and the Ugly

Every time I think I've seen it all, something else comes along and surprises me. I've picked out some of my favorite interview stories that I've learned from, and I use these scenarios when I'm preparing candidates for interviews. So while some people are confused when I prepare them for interviews with some of these situations, others get where the hints or *rules* are coming from and know there's a story behind my preparation for them.

From a dress code perspective, I've learned to spell out what not to wear to an interview. I want to lead with this because I've seen so many interviews go downhill before they've even started because of attire.

So, here are the things I tell people you cannot wear to interviews:

- T-shirts with profanity, cartoon characters, or brewery/alcohol logos
- Halloween costumes
- Santa costumes
- Moon Boots (the Napoleon Dynamite ones and the bouncy Nickelodeon kids trampoline shoes)
- Wedding dresses
- Dresses/shirts that you would wear out to a club on the weekend
- Shorts, flip flops, beach attire
- Hats, caps, beanies
- Sports attire

How about things you should not bring into an interview with you? Here's that list:

- Pets
- Concealed weapons of any kind
- Two liter bottles of soda
- First aid kit
- Make up bags (make up in a purse, totally ok. Makeup in a caboodle, no)
- Large amounts of food
- Duffel bags (like a gym bag)

I wish I was kidding when I listed these items, but I'm not. It would take me a very long time to cover each of these situations, but I'll highlight a few of my favorites. Several of them include a few of these items in one situation so, bonus!

A Bouncy Interview

I once met a candidate in a lobby just in time to see the Moon Boots they were sporting. These are the bouncy, personal trampoline shoes. This person was also decked out in sports attire and carrying a gym bag.

In their defense, they did tell me that they had a prior engagement that would make getting to the interview time a bit tight, but they would make it work. I didn't push it or clarify because the interview team couldn't make any other time slots work for the next few weeks, and I was driving the interview quickly as the candidate had told me they had other interviews scheduled.

The duffle bag that they were carrying consisted of interview appropriate clothes, and the candidate asked if they could change quickly before the interview. I messaged one of the team members and let them know to give me a few minutes to get the candidate in the interview room, and I'd message them when we were settled.

Why didn't I shut down the interview?

Well. The candidate did tell me they had something else going on leading up to the interview. Shame on me for not clarifying or trying to make a different time work that was more convenient for the candidate. Also, this was a niche skill set for a difficult to fill role. This candidate had already been technically screened, and I had spoken to them several times. They were an excellent applicant and did great in the interview. They just happened to show up in sports attire with bouncy shoes.

Now you may be wondering how the candidate drove in those shoes. They didn't. There was a park close by where they had been bouncing with friends, and then they hopped their way over to the interview with their bag in hand. It was harmless and we moved on. Although when we hired this person, I did tell them that part of their offer was contingent on teaching me how to use those shoes without breaking an ankle.

Santa Claus and Superman

In an agency we often walk candidates into an interview to introduce them to the hiring manager or interviewer. We would do this for a few reasons, the main one being that if a candidate didn't show up for the interview (happens often enough) we were at least there to apologize to the team.

Another reason is to catch things like a candidate wearing a Santa hat and coat to an interview. I had a candidate show up for an interview in a suit, but for their winter coat they wore a Santa suit jacket, and they had a Santa hat to complete the ensemble. It was early December, and I understand they were thinking that it would be a fun icebreaker for the interview; however, this was an incredibly professional environment and the company still observed a professional dress code at this time (yes, this was many years ago). The candidate was completely out of place.

I suggested the candidate place the hat and jacket in their car and strongly dissuaded them from wearing it into the interview. They politely declined and continued to wear the Santa attire to their interview. They did not get the job, and my client coached me on the qualities they were looking for in candidates.

Flash forward to October of the following year. Same client, different position. The candidate showed up in a Superman cape, ready for their interview on Halloween Day. I immediately told them what happened to the Santa candidate and suggested they remove the cape. They did, thankfully. I was not looking forward to the client scolding me again for having two candidates arrive wearing costumes! (What are the odds of this happening to the same client twice?!)

The second candidate also didn't get the job, but it was a technical skill gap rather than a costume this time. Although, the candidate did tell me that he told one of the interviewers that he had worn a cape for the holiday, and I made them remove it. So, who knows? Maybe it really was due to the cape after all.

One could say, shame on the client for not having a sense of humor. And, I agree. However, this is something that could absolutely prevent you from getting a job.

Pets, Snacks, and Attitudes

A few quick ones that include some of the others on the list, and then I'll get serious about some things that weren't completely ridiculous and do happen.

I've had candidates bring their dogs to the interview. One was a guide dog. Totally acceptable and they told me about it ahead of time. It was a non-issue. I had one candidate who brought their dog and left them in the car for a few minutes until their spouse could pick them up and take them home. I would have maybe made different arrangements, but it was fine.

The one that really takes the cake?

I had a candidate who brought a goldfish to an interview. They incorporated it into their interview discussing responsibility and how they were coaching their son to take responsibility for their pet as if it were a child. They explained that when their son was at school, he was responsible for finding someone to watch the fish. So, it was their day to watch the goldfish.

I understand what they were trying to do with both their son and the interview. It wasn't lost on me. Had that been a small part of the interview, it probably would have been fine. It wasn't a small part of the interview, however.

The candidate responded to almost all of the interview questions, relating back to the goldfish in some way, shape, or form. Fortunately, it was just a recruiter interview with me and not the entire interview team. I think I would have died of embarrassment if that would have happened.

Halfway through the conversation I tried redirecting the conversation away from the fish, who was very cute in its fishbowl, but did little to answer my questions about the candidate's technical ability to do their job.

I didn't move forward with the candidate in presenting them to my client and gave them the feedback that while the goldfish got their point across about accountability, responsibility, and leadership, it was the focal point of the entire conversation. I recommended that they maybe use some of those examples when they interview again, but leave the goldfish at home, and use some actual work examples to demonstrate how they portray those behaviors in the workplace.

This leads us to snacks in interviews.

For longer interviews I would have beverages and snacks in the room, and I would order breakfast, lunch, or dinner if the interview was close to or went over mealtimes. I once had a candidate that brought a lunch box cooler to their interview.

I was very confused when the candidate showed up to the interview fully loaded with a cooler. The interview was an hour and a half long, 9 to 10:30 a.m. I had beverages and snacks in the interview room already. The candidate said they were fine with their own snacks and proceeded to eat a full meal during the interview.

There are reasons that people would need to eat during an interview. Medical reasons that are none of my business whatsoever. This candidate did make sure to tell me that they weren't diabetic or anything, this was just the time of the day that they ate lunch because they woke up at 3 a.m. for work.

I understand having a routine, and if I had to wake up at 3 a.m., I'd probably be hungry at 9 a.m. too. If that's the case, however, I'd recommend suggesting other times for the interview. The interview team was perplexed at the complete four course meal that the candidate ate midmorning during the interview. The candidate didn't get the job.

The last example of out of the norm interviews I have for you is a candidate that had the absolute worst attitude. I had a phone screen with him and talked to him on the phone multiple times. By the time he came in for the interview it was like he was a different person.

This candidate who had interviewed well, had professional photos on their portfolio and had been nothing but professional and polite throughout our communications, showed up in attire that looked like he was ready to go to the club. Ripped jeans and a flashy, shiny button down shirt that looked made for the black lights of a discotheque.

The attitude that accompanied the outfit did little to help his case. The candidate rolled his eyes at the team's interview questions, sighed anytime they asked him to clarify, and talked down to the team. I would sit in on some of the technical interviews from time to time so that I could better learn the technology and what the team was looking for, and this just happened to be one that I sat in on part of the interview.

I was shocked at the candidate's behavior. He didn't want to be there. He did not want to interview. How this was the person that I had spoken to over the course of a few weeks is still beyond me.

I sent him a declination letter a few days later and got a thumbs up emoji response. I have no idea what happened that day. Per social media accounts, that person is still with the same employer, so the only reasoning I can come up with is that maybe he didn't want to change jobs, but had still applied and gone through with the interview. I really have no idea.

If you ever aren't feeling a job or a company, it's ok to withdraw from the interview process.

This leads to some examples of where things have gone wrong in interviews that are completely within the realm of normal possibilities.

When Interviews Go Wrong

I gave you some extreme examples of things that have happened to me while I was interviewing or had candidates interviewing with teams. Chat with any recruiter and they'll have similar experiences, I'm sure. Strange stuff happens.

Most of the time though, things just kind of go off the rails. Sometimes there are candidates that just interview better because they have more experience, are better prepared, or click with the team and the culture.

One of the most common reasons people don't nail an interview is they just don't have the experience that the position requires, or they don't thoroughly relay the experience that they have.

I had a candidate that was interviewing with the team and halfway through the interview, the manager messaged me through chat, and let me know that the candidate wasn't going to work out. They self-selected out. The questions that the team was asking around certain IT technologies weren't in their realm of expertise, and the candidate didn't feel comfortable with the role.

While this candidate self-selected out, most of us in this situation would try to navigate the questions to the best of our ability and flub our way through the interview. It's in our nature to not want to embarrass ourselves, so why wouldn't we try to make it through an interview? The team was so impressed with the candidate's honesty that they ended up hiring the person for another position that allowed room for training and development.

In most cases, candidates just weren't able to effectively answer the questions that were being asked. They either weren't able to relate their experience to what the team was looking for, or they didn't have the experience in their background.

In my years of recruiting, from what I have seen as a result of interviews, it is not that the candidates who have all of the experience get the jobs. It's the candidates who are able to think quickly, are prepared, and when they don't have the experience, they're able to articulate how they would approach the situation.

In short, leadership and communication skills are usually what lands the job. I have had candidates that were, on paper, the perfect fit. When they got to the interview, they weren't a good fit based on their lack of communication skills. They were flippant or gave short answers, they were uninterested in the position, or the team, or they were just unprofessional with how they spoke to people. I can count on one hand (ok, maybe two, I've been recruiting for a long time!) the number of times I put together an offer for a candidate who we were hiring purely based on their technical skills while simultaneously being concerned about their cultural fit. It does happen that a team decides to hire someone who they're concerned about fitting in, but they need the technical expertise, so they make a compromise. It's not the norm, but it does happen.

I have written hundreds of offers for candidates who were missing some technical piece of the requirements but were great communicators. They were ambitious, and they showed a desire to learn and grow. Attitude and aptitude will win the job nine times out of ten, and if a company wants to hire someone who can do the job but doesn't have the right attitude and doesn't fit in, do you even want to work there?

Ready for a few examples of times that an interviewer messed up?

Interviewer Blunders

I've interviewed thousands of people in my career. Some candidates stand out, others I wouldn't remember even if the candidate was standing in front of me. While I have many stories where the candidates absolutely stand out for interesting situations, as you've read above, I have some that are permanently stained on my brain because of something I did.

Remember when I said no Halloween costumes?

Well, there was a time that I had to interview candidates while dressed as Wonder Woman. I was head of the employee committee and had organized a costume contest for our corporate office. Other recruiters and HR people had decided that we would dress as superheroes. I was Wonder Woman.

I had made sure not to schedule interviews for that day, until I had to. I had a manager from overseas in the office that week to do interviews and based on some customer meetings, the only day that I could get the interviews in was the day that I was dressed head to toe as a superhero. I certainly felt like a superhero that day. Running around managing a contest, moving three candidates around for onsite interviews with the team, and making sure that everyone showed up in the right room and at the right time.

I had talked to the hiring manager and asked if he minded if I interviewed candidates in my superhero garb. To say he found it hilarious is an understatement, so I interviewed people in a cape and knee high boots. He also wanted to know how the candidates reacted when I greeted them in the lobby and brought them through the building dressed as WW.

Everyone reacted to it differently. I had one candidate who said, "Whoa!" and then said nothing else. One candidate asked me about it and joked that they left their costume at home. A third candidate absolutely loved it and showed me pictures of her dressed as WW a few years ago. The candidate who barely reacted did not do well in the interview. The other two did exceptionally well, and we ended up hiring both of those candidates.

The two who were amused by my costume also appreciated walking down the halls to see that everyone was in costume, that the conference rooms had been themed for Halloween, and that we also had team decorating contests going on for the office. They appreciated the culture and the camaraderie that they experienced in their short visit.

While it worked out fine, I still cringe when I think about my big hair and cape. I didn't have the best organizational skills at that moment, and my confidence was a bit shaky that day having to meet strangers while in a full costume.

I also had a situation where I had interviewed a candidate, we declined them, and then they surfaced again a few years later. The candidate remembered me; however, I did not remember them. They referenced our past conversation and even had the email that I had sent when we declined them.

Thank goodness we had a pleasant interaction, but I didn't remember anything. When I looked back at my notes, nothing triggered my memory. I was at a complete loss with this candidate (which is not usual for recruiters, we remember everything!). I was off my game, and I know I was asking the same questions that I probably had asked them the last time since they were interviewing for a similar role, but I didn't remember interviewing them. Thankfully, I had my previous notes, so I could ask them to refresh my memory on a situation that we had previously discussed or to discuss their experience since we last spoke.

At the end of the conversation the candidate called me out and asked me if I remembered them. I confessed that I didn't, apologized, and relayed the information to the manager. The manager had notes on the candidate too, and the interview had not gone well. Not only did I feel dumb for not remembering this candidate, but I put them through another interview when there was no way the hiring manager would revisit this candidate. I wasted their time and mine.

Other mistakes I've made during an interview include the following:

- Accidentally shut my computer down, and lost their resume and my notes
- Deleted a candidate's presentation that they had prepared for an interview (they had a backup copy fortunately)
- My phone battery died in the middle of a conversation
- Forgot what I was saying mid-sentence and had to come back to it
- Called the candidate the wrong name
- Forgot what position I was interviewing a candidate for

- Lost reception while trying to interview someone while I was driving
- Spilled coffee and burned myself badly
- Lost a shoe walking a candidate to an interview room
- Tripped and fell down a set of stairs while walking a candidate to a room
- Got the hiccups for almost 20 minutes
- Choked on my own spit while talking and proceeded to red face gag and cough for five minutes

I'm really not accident prone. I'm just a normal person that has interviewed a lot of people and eventually life happens to us all. I don't get nervous interviewing people anymore, but hiring managers get nervous. Recruiters or interviewers that have situations like I listed above, get nervous.

I had someone interview me who told me they were so nervous to interview someone that interviews for a living. I've coached hundreds of managers over the years on how to interview and so many of them would share that they were nervous. They were afraid of saying the wrong thing or asking the wrong questions. Most hiring managers are afraid of making the wrong decision.

I've told candidates who I'm coaching that most of the time the interviewers are just as afraid of you as you are of them. Have a conversation with them and share your experience with them. Maybe you're not a perfect fit, but a well prepared, communicative, and confident candidate is in a much better position than a candidate who is unprepared and scared!

Chapter 9: Trials and Tribulations of Recruiters. The Things You Don't See.

I would love to tell you that the lifecycle for a job is this:

- Hiring Manager identifies need for a position
- Recruiter posts position
- Candidates apply
- Recruiter interviews candidates
- Hiring manager and teams interview candidates
- Recruiter makes offer
- Candidate accepts offer
- Everyone lives happily ever after

In a perfect world, this is how we would roll and every position would only be open for as long as it takes to get the candidates through the process. There are so many things that come up and impact the process though. All of these things are out of your control, and most of them are out of the control of the recruiter as well.

Changing Requirements

This one happens a lot. Ideally, a hiring manager identifies a role that they need to fill on their team, and they use a company job description template to set the requirements for the job. However, what often happens is that the company job description is cookie cutter and either way too specific (ruling out candidates who should be considered qualified) or way too generic (everyone ends up being qualified).

Also, managers don't always know what they want or need for a position. There have been too many times to count where a manager and I meet, discuss the requirements of the role, and then when we're interviewing they are mentioning requirements that are not on the job description, and they never shared with me.

I had a manager tell me once, "I'll know what I need once I see it."

As a recruiter we guide and coach managers as to what they need in a position, what the market looks like for their talent pool and their expectations. I have told people that they are looking for a "Unicorn" so many times I named my company after this very scenario. No matter how much we coach and lead, we ultimately do not make the final hiring decision… as much as we would like to and probably should sometimes.

If you've ever seen a job posting that you applied to a few months ago, and it just looks ever so slightly different now? Probably a recruiter is trying to hit a moving target.

From my experience, this happens more often in the following scenarios:

- Micromanagement cultures where managers are afraid of making the wrong choices
- Inexperienced managers
- Startups that are trying to cover multiple positions in one

If you've ever applied to a job and were sitting in the interview process only to have them listing a bunch of different responsibilities and technical abilities that weren't in the job description, you are interviewing for an ever changing role that they are having trouble defining. If you're ok with ambiguity, pursue it. If not, don't take it personally if you get a decline letter. It's not you.

The Mystery Candidate

This has happened to me in both agency and in house recruiting. We'd be interviewing, and I'd think we were close to closing up a position when all of a sudden, the manager would have a candidate that came out of nowhere.

When I was in an agency, I was a little more used to this because I understood that they had internal candidates, referrals, and other agency and internal recruiters working on a role. I just always assumed that the internal recruiter was in the loop, and the information just wasn't rolling down to me.

As an internal recruiter, I learned that's not always the case.

There were way too many times when the hiring manager all of a sudden had a candidate from an agency that hadn't run through the proper recruiting process, or there was a referral candidate that someone sent them, and they interviewed them around me. It's not right, and it's not following a fair process, but it does happen.

If a recruiter tells you they had another candidate that they moved forward with, and you had asked during the process if they had any other candidates, and the recruiter said no, this might be what happened. Or, if you have a final, final interview, and you're sure the job is yours, this might be the case.

There are numerous other things that could have happened, but this has happened to me quite a few times, and I couldn't sell out the hiring manager or team so I'd have to tell the candidate that they were being declined because another candidate had come through who was stronger. This is true, but I just wasn't in the loop about it.

Really, Really Long Interview Processes

Ask any recruiter and they are going to tell you that they hate it when there are seven step interview processes. I would be very surprised to find any recruiter that said that this many steps were necessary.

Recruiters are assessed on specific metrics:

- Time to fill
- Quality of candidates/submittals
- Candidate pipeline
- Number of fills

There are others, but these are the ones that are directly related to how long the process takes.

If a recruiter doesn't have candidates in their pipeline who can do the job, they are out hunting for qualified candidates. For agencies especially, they are held to specific metrics tied to how many people they meet in a week, how many candidates they submit to open positions, how many of those candidates are interviewed, and how many people they hire each year.

Recruiters are hustling to fill positions. The time to fill metric means how long it takes for the recruiter to fill a position. In hourly positions, it's common to see goals of 15-30 days time to fill metrics whereas office professional positions are usually in the 45-60 days range.

When you look at a company that has multiple interview steps, it becomes more difficult for the recruiter to meet those metrics. We also know that you don't need to meet with a candidate numerous times to know if they're the right fit for the role.

Remember the situations that I mentioned before with changing requirements and micromanagement and inexperienced managers? This is also most likely the case when it comes to really lengthy interview processes. Teams or companies that have the whole company interview often have a hard time making decisions or coming to agreement.

My recommendation was always:

- Recruiter phone screen
- Hiring Manager and HR Interview
- Team member (s) interview (no more than two people)
- One-over manager *

*I only recommended one-over manager interviews for management and above level roles. When it gets to Sr. Director or Executive level roles, it's going to be a lengthy process and the whole world will be involved. However, for the rest of the positions that most of us are going to be interviewing for, we don't need to meet the entire team, the other teams, and the leadership team.

I've coached numerous clients who are heartbroken who haven't gotten a position after going through seven or eight interview steps. Again, this isn't on you. Don't take it personally. This is a company that doesn't trust one another or themselves.

Non-Responsive Hiring Managers

Ahh, hiring managers that don't respond. This is another situation that I always thought just happened to agency recruiters. Working in an agency, I was accustomed to working hard to get candidates submitted to the hiring manager only to not receive a response for weeks. Sure there are tricks, like setting up a debrief meeting after the interviews or sending calendar invites to remind the manager to send feedback, but they'd just ignore it.

When I moved to an in-house recruiting position I thought, this is great! We're going to interview and make hiring decisions within 24 hours and things are going to move.

I was so, so wrong.

What I learned was hiring managers often hired agencies for recruiting when they struggled with a particular position or their recruiting team was overloaded. So while some of them would *ghost* me and not get back to me after submitting candidates or after they had interviewed my candidates, they still tended to be more invested and engaged in the process.

When I moved to the corporate recruiting world, I learned that hiring is a small part of what a hiring manager does, and they don't always excel at it, and oftentimes, they don't enjoy it. Even if they were working double the amount of hours to keep things afloat, they would do that before responding about my candidates or sending feedback.

I often would tell them, "Help me help you."

Unless the manager is a recruiting manager, hiring is only a very small part of their job. I would send meeting invites and set up times for us to talk about candidates and interviews, and they would decline the meeting, reschedule it, or no show.

It wasn't all of the managers, and it wasn't all of the time, but if a business need came up that would be prioritized before interviewing.

I followed the three strikes and then you're out rule with my managers after a while if they couldn't respond to me.

After three attempts to contact them to get feedback, I'd tell them they had two business days to respond to me or I'd put their position on hold. A week after a requisition was put on hold I'd email them and tell them they had one more week before I canceled it.

I canceled a lot of requisitions in my time.

I also did this with candidate feedback. I'd make up excuses twice for a manager. After the third time I had to follow up with a candidate to tell them I didn't have feedback, I'd tell them the truth.

"I'm sorry but I have been unable to get feedback or a response from the hiring manager."

I'd tell the hiring manager in my warning emails that this was going to happen, and I was going to tell the candidate they weren't responding. I still had managers that wouldn't respond, and I'd cancel their requisition and apologize to the candidates.

I had been a recruiter for quite a few years at this point and was in a position where I could make these types of calls. Most recruiters are not in that position so they make up excuses for the hiring manager, or they stop following up with candidates because they don't know what to do anymore.

Again, it's not you. This is an "us" problem.

Internal Candidates

Have you gone through an entire interview process only to find out that the company went with an internal candidate?

You're left sitting there wondering why the heck they even interviewed you and feel like they wasted your time.

Sometimes this happens. You have hiring managers that want to compare candidates. (I feel this is not the right way to interview, but that's a topic for another day.) The recruiter is tasked with finding a few candidates for the manager to compare to the internal candidate. This is bad news all the way around, but managers still do it.

It is possible that you were just a comparison candidate, and they were just shopping around to see if they could find someone stronger than the internal candidate. Imagine being that internal candidate knowing they are interviewing external candidates to try and find someone better than you! This happened to me once. I was the internal candidate while the team interviewed multiple external candidates trying to find someone better than me for the role. It doesn't feel great, and often HR and recruiters try to persuade the team to make a decision quickly for the internal candidate's sake. (I was the backup candidate for six months!)

To meet posting requirements, and to maintain US hiring policies, also post internally and externally for a set amount of days and review and consider any candidates that meet the requirements. This can lead to the perception from candidates that the hiring manager is shopping around when in fact they are just interviewing all qualified candidates.

Another situation that often happened to me is that we'd be interviewing candidates for a while, and then an internal candidate somewhere else, on another team, would resign. In an attempt to retain them, we would offer them other open positions somewhere else in the company. I moved people around quite a bit during the Great Resignation era just a few years ago.

Someone would resign, and instead of writing an offer to the external candidate who we just spent interviewing for the last few weeks, we moved an internal candidate into the role.

It's possible that the internal candidates aren't qualified, and the manager is interviewing them because they're internal, and while they don't meet the requirements, they have internal knowledge of how the company runs. Sometimes internal candidates get the roles because it's career development and growth, or because they have company experience that will help them overcome a skills gap.

Budget Cuts, Lost Financing

Sometimes everything goes smoothly. We're at the finish line and someone somewhere decides the position isn't needed, or the company is not going to fill the position to cut costs. I usually preferred this rather than laying off people that were already employed with us, but it still wasn't fun to call a candidate, and tell them we were canceling a position. I know as a candidate it's incredibly frustrating!

Another situation that I've had happen too many times to count is we were in the middle of an interview process, and leadership didn't realize that a position had even been opened. Once they caught wind of a position floating out there that they hadn't approved or been aware of, they shut it down until the position had been fully vetted. The team didn't follow the proper approval process, and they lost the position.

There are a multitude of hurdles that recruiters face when they're trying to fill positions. You can bet that the recruiter will do what they can to influence the process and get things moving, but there's a lot of variables out of their control.

Chapter 10: Salary Negotiations, The Do's and Don'ts.

Salary negotiations have changed over the years. When I started recruiting, prior to the 2009 recession, very rarely did I see negotiations. Some, but not many. Beginning in 2009 I never saw salary negotiations. People had been out of work for quite a while sometimes, or they were preparing to lose their jobs so they took whatever was offered to them. In a few years things were relatively back to normal. Salary negotiations happened occasionally, but people were negotiating for a few thousand dollars or a few days of additional paid time off (PTO).

During the Great Resignation (2021-2022), the negotiations were out of this world. People were negotiating for astronomical salaries, and in a lot of cases, they were getting them. I was quite shocked by some of the negotiations I was handling and after over a decade in recruiting, I was beginning to question my negotiating skills as a recruiter. Fortunately it seems that things have rebounded a bit, and negotiations are much more reasonable again!

With negotiations, there are a few things that I recommend people do and then a few things I'd caution against in your negotiations.

Do:

- Research what salaries look like in your area for your skill set

- Be upfront about your salary expectations
- Know your bottom line
- Be confident in your negotiations
- Be realistic
- Thank the employer for the offer

And here are a few things I recommend you don't do.

Don't

- Ask for salary or benefits unrealistically higher than the range you gave the recruiter/manager
- Inflate your current salary
- Negotiate if you aren't comfortable doing so
- Decline offers too quickly
- Accept too quickly
- Negotiate before receiving the written offer
- Leverage an offer with a company to get a raise at your current company

Ok, so how should we go about negotiating an offer? Do we have to negotiate?

Do I Negotiate?

You don't always need to.

I've had numerous candidates through the years who have said, "I know I'm supposed to negotiate, but I want this job, and I'm happy with the offer."

Great. If you're happy with the offer and don't want the stress of negotiating. Don't.

I am not a negotiator for myself. When I've received an offer, I either accepted or didn't. I didn't want the stress of it, and I didn't feel that I could be confident negotiating for myself. I can negotiate on behalf of my candidates all day long, but for myself it was a different story, and I followed my own advice. I didn't feel confident negotiating, so I didn't.

A lot of people think they will be judged negatively if they don't negotiate. I don't believe that's always true. When a candidate gave me a salary range, and we were able to exceed what they were looking for and give them extra perks they weren't planning on, I wasn't surprised when they didn't negotiate.

Sometimes employers know a candidate's worth, they want them, and they give them a really good offer.

Feel good about it, accept it, and enjoy your new position!

If you aren't confident about negotiating, then don't. Here's what I've coached candidates to say when they didn't receive an offer that they liked, and they didn't feel comfortable negotiating.

"When we discussed salary expectations during the interview process, I mentioned I was looking for X salary. I look forward to hearing the next steps."

If you discussed the salary up front in the interview process (and this should always, always happen), and the offer comes in lower than what was discussed, sharing a gentle reminder with the recruiter should be enough without you having to compromise what you were looking for and making yourself uncomfortable negotiating.

As a recruiter, I will straight out tell you that I knew when I was making a garbage offer. And I hated it. Recruiters will fight and plead with the team to get you the salary that you're asking for. We don't have control over it 99% of the time. There's the hiring manager, human resources, and compensation/finance people who all have input and more control than the recruiter does.

So, don't shoot the messenger. Remind them what you told them you wanted, and I can tell you that the recruiter is going back to the team and saying this:

"I told you what they were looking for. It wasn't this offer. They want us to match X amount."

If there is an internal or agency recruiter who doesn't do that, you probably don't want to work there. I know a lot of people believe that internal recruiters do their best to get top talent for low ball salaries. Maybe some do, but most of us want to build strong, talented teams. We're the ones making bad offers when the team puts them together, and we don't like it either. We are constantly talking to people, and we know what the market looks like and the value that people can bring. We also don't want to keep recruiting for revolving door positions. It's not a good look for the company, and we don't like trying to sell roles that we know are going to be open again in six months.

Do Your Research, Know Your Bottom Line

A few internet searches, and you can find salary ranges in your area for your skill set. If you're part of groups or organizations (which you should be, remember our networking discussion!), they will most likely have some information for you as well.

When I research rates for a skill set, I will often take the ranges of the salaries that I'm finding online and do an average.

For example:

Project Manager Salaries

- LinkedIn: $110k
- Indeed: $90k
- Glassdoor: $95k

295,000/3 = $98,333

I would recommend to my client to anticipate a range of $90-110k but to budget for $120k to cover any negotiations or if there was a niche skill that was required. As a recruiter, I would target salary ranges of $95-105k when looking for candidates. As a candidate, I'd recommend targeting around $100k (who asks for $98,333??).

This is a basic example not accounting for niche skill sets, niche industries, experience, or geographic challenges. Salary can change, and it will, based on all the things I mentioned above. Doing your research will help you to better understand if you're being underpaid, or if you're compensated well and might face challenges finding comparable salaries.

I've had candidates that were living in one geographic location and working remotely for a company in another location. Some companies have different ranges for different areas (most do) so the odds that you'll be paid based on where you live is likely, which is great if you live in a major metropolitan area. You'll be paid based on where you live. If you live in a low cost of living area, don't expect to be paid a range based on a large metropolitan area. It could happen, but it's unlikely.

This brings us to knowing your bottom line.

If you have a rough range of what your skill set is paid in your particular area, the next part of the equation is your own personal needs.

Your bottom line doesn't have to be just a dollar amount. For me, being remote was my bottom line. I left a company and took a pay cut to be remote and work from home. For some people, having a higher salary is worth more to them because they're saving for a kid's college fund, or they support their parents or others.

It's ok if money is your bottom line. It's ok if your bottom line is a good culture, a strong manager, being remote, and having Fridays off, etc. Know what your bottom line is, and feel comfortable with it.

We also have a bottom line to pay our expenses! If a job has full benefits, Fridays off, and it's remote, but we can't pay our bills, then we need to look for something else! Know what it takes to cover your expenses.

I've known multiple people that have left jobs after a few months, stating low pay. They gave us a range, we made an offer in that range, and they accepted only to discover that they couldn't cover their basic living expenses.

How does that happen?!

Well, they were willing to take a lower salary because of something else - a shorter commute, a better schedule, etc., but they didn't take into consideration their budget and what they needed to live. Whoops.

Be Up Front and Be Realistic

Ok, so do you bring up the salary, or do you wait for the recruiter to do it?

The recruiter should be asking on the first phone screen. They don't have time to waste and neither do you. If I looked at someone's resume and knew there was probably zero way I could afford to hire this person, I'd ask right away.

If they don't ask, then you can ask about the salary range.

I recommend you ask questions about the role, the company, and the culture first. You should be given time at the end of the conversation to ask questions, if you aren't already having an open, back and forth conversation with the recruiter. Ask all of your questions first and then ask:

"This sounds like a great opportunity and I'm very interested in moving forward. Are you able to confirm the salary range so we know if we're in the same realm?"

Asking them to confirm the range is a much more comfortable way of asking, "What are you paying for this role?" However, many people will just ask this too!

Be up front when they ask you what you're making, and don't overinflate what you're making if you feel comfortable enough sharing. Some companies do verify compensation info in the final screening processes, and you don't want to be caught lying about your compensation.

Include your total compensation expectations. Salary, bonus incentives, stipends, health benefits (especially if they are one of the 100% employer paid programs!), reimbursements, etc. I've had candidates that had out of this world health benefits that we couldn't touch, but we bumped up their compensation to cover the difference. There are things that companies can do if you're up front about what you're looking for, but if you don't tell them, they won't know, and you won't get a comparable offer.

Also, be realistic about what you're asking for.

I've had plenty of candidates come back and ask for $30k, $40k, $70k more than the range they told me!

WHAT?!

I've also had candidates tell me that their salary range was $90-100k (for example). We offered $100k, at the top of their range. They countered for $170k!

Ouch.

They didn't get $170k, and at that point, they didn't get $100k. We declined the counter offer and stood by our offer. They called our bluff, and we went with our runner-up candidate who was fabulous! Maybe there were other factors that influenced their counter offer, but they weren't discussing it with us so there was very little we could do. We couldn't match a salary of $170k that was about $55k outside of our range.

This same scenario with varying degrees of shock has happened to me throughout my entire career. In one case I had a student, right out of college, who asked for $70k (reasonable for an engineer), and then when we offered, countered for $120k. That was more than what half of our team who had been there for several years were making!

It's ok to negotiate for a bit more than what was offered, within the range that you previously discussed with them; however, this came out of nowhere and lost the candidate the job. Your negotiation should be fair and realistic and not so far out of reach that the offer is rescinded.

Accepting, Declining and Leveraging Offers

When do you accept? When do you decline? How do you decline gracefully?

Recruiters will try to push for a verbal offer. They're trained to get you on the line right away because people are unlikely to come back and decline if they've already given you a verbal acceptance. Or at least it used to be like that.

It's called a lock down. Recruiters do this throughout the process. They get you hooked, confirm your expectations, and hammer out the details over and over again so there's nothing left for you to do but accept.

The recruiters reading this won't like this, but I'm saying this anyway.

Do not verbally accept an offer before you've reviewed it in writing. Never, ever.

Don't try to negotiate an offer before you have it in writing, and don't accept it before you've reviewed the written offer.

Review the benefits and the bonus structure, if there is one. Review the non-disclosure agreement, the employment agreement, and any other agreements that the company has such as paid time off, sick leave, and medical leave, etc.

I've seen recruiters lock down a candidate, and get them to agree to an offer on the phone, before they've received the benefits and reviewed the compensation structure. The candidate then went off and read through the offer and benefits packages and came back with a ton of questions, negotiations and concerns. They knew they agreed to an offer that didn't meet their bottom line and now they were all in an awkward situation.

My approach?

I prefer a conversation with the candidate. I would go through benefits with them, explain the premiums and max out of pocket costs. I talked through PTO and holiday pay. I would explain the bonus structure and how they could be successful and hit targets. I talked through the salary. We discussed hybrid vs. remote, and if they were traveling or driving in, what that commute would look like. Also, what the hours and expectations were for overtime work.

By this point in our relationship (we had been through the interview process together and now the offer discussion), candidates would tell me what their concerns were, or if they had other offers they were waiting on. I would learn where we ranked in terms of offers, or if there was something we could do to make the offer better. We had a conversation and I let the candidate review the documents after our call. They could call, text, or email me with questions, and I gave them space.

Why don't I force candidates to give me a verbal acceptance?

Because I don't want anyone to shortchange themselves and not give them time to make sure that the offer is the best for their situation. Whether I was an agency recruiter or in-house, I didn't want someone to take a job they weren't happy with. As an agency recruiter, if someone backed out or quit, I'd have to replace them and/or pay back fees that I had been paid. In-house, I'd have to recruit the position again, and the team would be frustrated that they had wasted time training someone just to have to turn around and hire again. Not fun for anyone.

Why force someone into a role where the offer isn't what they want, or it isn't the right role for them?

I don't want to lock anyone down into a role or situation that isn't good for them. This is their life and career. They get the opportunity to make sure it's the right decision for them.

Ok, that said, it's not a great idea to not accept an offer just because you're using it to leverage another offer somewhere else. Recruiters and companies can tell when this is happening. Back and forth negotiations when the company has met requirements of a counter, and there continues to be more negotiations, or a candidate goes quiet for a while. We know, and it can burn your bridge with that company.

If you're going to use an offer at one company to negotiate an offer with another company, respectfully decline the offer at the company that you know you're not going to accept. If you're just trying to drive each company up to the highest end of their range, you're playing a risky game. I'd encourage you to do some self reflection to determine which company will meet your non-monetary needs. Don't sell yourself short, but money won't make up for a role that doesn't fulfill your career growth. Not long term, at least.

Ok, let's look at some of the different parts of an offer and what goes into it in the next chapter.

Chapter 11: The Behind the Scenes

I once made an offer to a candidate who was incredibly strong. We found an excellent candidate, they interviewed well, and they shared what their current salary was.

We were going to be able to give this candidate a $20k raise in base AND a 15% annual bonus. Also, additional PTO, better health benefits, and relocation assistance to help them get back to their hometown.

I was proud of the offer. The candidate was thrilled! They went to review the offer, and we were going to follow up the next day. The candidate did have another offer that they were waiting on, but didn't think it was going to compare to what we had offered.

The next day the candidate called me… in shock. They had received an offer that met or exceeded all the areas of our offer. I knew I could play with a bonus and salary so I still felt ok about matching what they had.

Then they told me that the sign-on bonus was in the form of a down payment on a house that was something they didn't think they would be able to afford for at least a few years. They talked to me about the company and the opportunity. I congratulated them and wished them well. We couldn't match it, and we couldn't offer them the same level of opportunity, at the present moment, as what they were being offered.

When I told the hiring manager and my HR partner what had happened, we shrugged it off. What can you do about that? We weren't in a position to compete with the offer, and the candidate had a great opportunity with the other company.

It became a running inside joke among this team and my recruiting team.

When I'd ask my team about the offers that they had out to candidates that we were waiting to hear back on, I'd ask them if they thought we'd be negotiating any down payments on houses.

Good for that candidate, and I truly hope that the role was great! They earned it!

Now, the behind the scenes question, why weren't we in a position to meet the huge sign-on bonus?

Behind the Scenes of an Offer

As candidates when we receive an offer, unless we're in HR, we don't always know what goes on from the time of our interview to the time that we're being presented an offer.

Often, offers are put together by some assembly of HR, recruiting, compensation, and finance personnel, and then routed for approval by the team. The candidate's experience and their salary expectations are taken into account, but the other major factors that come into play in the offer process are internal equity and pay scales.

Every position is graded, and there is a salary range attached to that position whether it's an hourly position or salaried position. Recruiters are given a salary range and look for candidates that meet the requirements and are within the graded salary range. Several states have laws that require companies to post their salary ranges for jobs in an effort to create pay transparency.

Internal equity stems from the fact that there are other people in this same position in the company making a certain salary based on their qualifications and time spent in the company. In an effort to keep pay fair, companies try not to bring in people from outside the company with less experience at a higher salary level than what their current employees are making in the same role.

Does it happen, though?

All the time.

However, with the exception of 2021-2022, the times that I had to bring in an external candidate with less experience than an internal candidate, at a higher salary, was few and far between. I could count the number of times on one hand. With the hiring boom of 2021 and 2022, this became more and more common, as did resignations.

As an internal recruiter, very rarely did I run into situations where we didn't know the candidate's expectations when we were making an offer. However, when it came to negotiations, and they started countering for things that were higher than the range that they had given us, that's when it became more complicated.

Whether it be other offers or counteroffers from a current company, once the negotiations got up to the point where they were higher than what we discussed throughout the course of our conversations, we either couldn't meet them and held firm with a final offer, or in some cases, we rescinded the offer.

Sign-On Bonuses, Stock Awards, Extras

Sign-on bonuses were always a quick way for me to ensure a candidate got what they were looking for if we couldn't meet their salary expectations to their fullest. At higher leveled positions it's more common for sign-on bonuses to be a part of the offer. The cash up front is great for the candidate, but there is incentive for the company as well. Most cash sign-on bonuses require the new hire to stay in their position for 12-24 months (I've seen as short as 3 months and as high as 36 months), or they risk having to pay some of it back.

How does this work, and do you accept an offer with a sign-on bonus?

I had one candidate tell me that they weren't planning on staying with the company longer than a year and that this was just a filler job until they found something else. They declined the offer. I've had other candidates accept the offer and then resign within the window of repayment; however, one candidate was a military spouse and had to relocate, and another had medical issues. We didn't ask them to repay the bonuses. I have seen cases where companies have required payment and others where they decided it would be more work than what it's worth and didn't seek repayment. It's a risk that you take if you are unsure of a company, job, manager, etc.

When bonuses are paid you net a percentage of the bonus after taxes are taken out, so you could very well be asked to pay back a percentage of the bonus based on gross, not on the net. If you are excited about the company and the role, take the bonus, and start your new journey! Often in the event of termination or downsizing, you would not be asked to repay the bonus as the termination was no fault of yours. Therefore, unless you don't plan on being with the company within the allotted payback period, enjoy the bonus!

Remember how I said I used sign-on bonuses to meet a candidate's salary requirements?

If a candidate wanted a $100k salary, but I could only offer $95k due to other factors, I could get approval to get the candidate a $5k sign-on bonus, bringing the compensation up to $100k for the first year.

But what about year two?

Ask about the company's performance review and salary wage raise policies. If you're starting in the third or fourth quarter of the year, it's possible that you won't qualify for a raise the following year. Most companies prorate raises as well so if you start in

February, you might only qualify for a raise based on 10 months in the company for that performance review year.

If you're ok with a slight dip in income in year two, or stagnate compensation, as long as you're getting a fair offer and feel good about it, go for it! No one likes surprises, especially when it comes to your income, so just make sure you know what your year two compensation will be based on.

In companies that offer internal equity, stock awards, stock purchase plans, etc., you may be eligible for an initial award at the time of offer. Ask for the vesting schedule and the plan information so that you know when your awards will be vested, and what happens should you leave the company. Also, in the case of an employee stock purchase plan, you'll want to know when and how much you're able to purchase and what the rate is.

With an offer grant, you'll want to make sure you know when the official grant date is (usually around your start date), so you know what the cost per share is. The offer letter will share either the dollar amount, or the number of shares, and the date of the grant will help you to know the price per share if given a number of shares.

Stock awards are also a negotiable item in your offer. You can negotiate for a higher amount of awards, but vesting dates are usually non-negotiable. Review the vesting schedule and what happens if you leave the company before your awards are vested. (In most cases, you will forfeit the remaining shares.)

This leaves us to the extras in an offer. Car allowances, phone allowances, internet stipends, PTO, health insurance premiums, gym memberships, etc.

I have worked with companies that offered car and phone allowances based on the position. This is something that is based on company policy, and the type of role you're being offered. What's common for a sales position is not going to be common for an engineer, for example.

I mention this as I have negotiated quite a few offers where candidates wanted their car paid for or mileage into the office reimbursed (for an onsite position). These are often items you cannot negotiate, with PTO being a potential exception.

When it comes to PTO, there might be some wiggle room. Might.

At higher levels, director and executive level roles, PTO is often considerably higher than it would be for an individual contributor or new manager level role. For individual contributor and management roles, when I first started recruiting I rarely saw more than two weeks of PTO offered. Now, between two to three weeks is more common.

If you are coming from a role that offers more PTO than what the new company is offering, you may be able to negotiate some based on your level and experience. Oftentimes, PTO is awarded based on years of service, but when you're moving to the new company, your previous experience may be taken into consideration when your PTO is determined.

If you're looking for something to improve in your offer, and if you're being offered the company's starting PTO rate versus one based on your experience and tenure in your profession, PTO might be an area that you can negotiate more easily than salary or bonuses.

Chapter 12: Post Acceptance. You Got the Job! What Do You Do Now?

Congratulations! You've applied, networked, interviewed, negotiated, and finally accepted!

Now what?

Leaving Your Current Employer Gracefully

Hopefully you're only leaving your company for professional growth and are on good terms. However, it's quite possible that you've had a terrible experience and can't stand your boss or management, or something has gone terribly, terribly wrong.

I hope not, but if this is the case, you should still give a two weeks' notice and professionally hand off your work.

I understand why people don't give notices—an employer can term you for no good reason and without any notice. Why can't we do the same?

Well, because of your coworkers. The people around you who still have to work there after you leave and will now be taking on your responsibilities. Hand things off to them, and keep things cordial and professional.

You never know who might move to another company and be in a hiring capacity or be asked by a recruiter if they should hire you. This goes back to our networking discussion earlier. Keeping professional relationships positive will help you in the future.

Turn in your equipment, say goodbye to coworkers, and make sure to exchange information with those you want to stay in contact with. You'll want HR's contact information in case you need it for tax purposes later on, or if you need information on 401k rollovers, or any other final transfer information.

It can be very tempting to tell anyone that you didn't get along with what you think of them or to withhold information, but in the end, it won't help you close the chapter and move on as easily as you might think. Trust me, I've had to be talked out of rage quitting several times throughout my career. I listened to advice, left professionally, and have had networking opportunities arise several times with people who I enjoyed working with. It's worth it to leave professionally.

If you're leaving for advancement, relocation, better hours, or pay, etc., then it should be no problem to leave gracefully!

Counter Offers

Another thing that happens quite often while you're negotiating your next great opportunity is that your current employer counters when you turn in your resignation.

You were leaving for better pay, better hours, or a career advancement, and all of a sudden here is your current employer with everything you've ever wanted.

What do you do??

I'd be shocked if you found a recruiter that told you to accept it. We see it time and time again where an employee tries to grow in their current company and strives for better pay or advancement, and they are told no at least once, if not several times. Then, once the employee has a shiny new offer at another company, all of a sudden their current employer swoops in with everything they've ever wanted.

Don't take it.

The reasons that you want to leave aren't going to change. You may get the title or the salary that you want this time, but what about the next time you're looking for advancement? The odds that you are being offered the last role that you will ever want in your career are slim. You'll want advancement and raises again, and if your company only makes that happen when they're faced with losing you, it's not going to be a long-term fit.

Leaving for a bad culture or bad manager?

I see this a lot too. Candidates tell me they can't stand working for their manager or leadership is poor all the way around. There's a nightmare coworker that is dead weight to the team, but they won't get rid of them. Then they receive an offer and decide to resign, and their company bribes them with lucrative financial incentives to stay.

Don't take it.

The things you didn't like about your manager, company, or coworker aren't going to change. Money doesn't make a bad boss or bad company tolerable for that much longer. Maybe the money makes it worthwhile for six more months, but it doesn't make the problems go away.

Recruiters see it all the time. All. The. Time. Every candidate I've had who has declined my offer and taken a counter offer with their current employer was back out on the market shortly. In an agency, it's easier to keep track of when they're back in the market because they'd reach out to me again saying, "You were right… I'm on the market again." However, even as a corporate recruiter, I've had candidates reach back out and tell me that they would be interested in exploring roles with our company if we're still interested in them.

Onboarding for Your New Role

Once you've accepted an offer you'll have a series of events that you'll need to make sure you stay on top of so you don't delay your start date at your new company

Within the United States, it's common to have to take a drug screen within several days of an accepted offer. This part is critical as a delay to take the drug test could result in a rescinded offer (worst case scenario), or a delayed start date (best case). With some states and companies allowing different levels and having different laws for some drugs, make sure you know what the company policy is. This information is usually given shortly after the time of offer and is in an employee handbook or in the drug screen information itself.

My best advice for this?

If you are a THC proponent, dry out before interviewing and accepting an offer. Just because it's legal in a state doesn't mean that the company you are applying to permits it. Some companies disclose their drug testing policies on their website or in their job descriptions. If this is something that could be an issue for you, I'd suggest just following my advice here and drying out during your job search. Then, I'd recommend following their drug policy because you could be tested during your employment, or if you have an accident on your work site.

I've seen quite a few people lose their dream job over a joint.

In tandem with a drug screen is often a background check. This is also something that is critical to kick off as soon as you receive the information because it could take a few weeks for the background checks to come back, depending on what the company screens for, and depending on the city/county you live in. Some counties take longer than others.

Do you have a really common name or one with a lot of aliases? Is it summer and your education needs to be verified? Is your degree from out of the country? Have you moved a lot, and had multiple jobs or a past employer is now closed?

These items could all take longer to verify, therefore getting your background check information in as quickly as possible can help prevent your background check from delaying your start date.

If you do have hiccups, having copies of your W2 from past employers, or a copy of your diploma or transcripts, might resolve some of those issues.

And what about a criminal record that's maybe not so clean?

In most cases, as long as the infraction isn't related to the job or doesn't impede your ability to work for the company, you're probably ok. You can't have a conviction for grand theft auto, but apply to be a truck driver (yes, I had this once), but there are plenty of other jobs you could apply to that wouldn't be related to that particular infraction.

Update Your Professional Sites

It's your first day, and you've started your new role!

It's common to abandon your professional social media sites once you've landed your new job, but it's important you update your information to reflect your new position.

Your employer will appreciate it and from a networking standpoint, you never know who might want to come work with you or for you! Or, after a year in your new role, maybe someone wants to snag you from the company to move you into your dream job! As a recruiter, I can tell you that we often target specific companies and skill sets so showing others where you are may help you continue to advance your career!

Quite a few companies offer referral programs too! If someone is looking at your company for their next opportunity, they won't reach out to you if you aren't listed at their target company. Update your profile so your professional network knows where you landed and let the networking begin!

You've made it! Enjoy the new role!

Chapter 13: Some of the Best Post Acceptance Debacles

So once someone accepts the role, it's all said and done, right?

Recruiters will tell you that we never consider a role truly filled until someone has been in the role for six months, and even then, we're cautiously optimistic.

It doesn't happen extremely often, but it's happened enough that I have sleepless nights the night before someone is expected to start a new job. You just never know if they will show up or not!

Ok, so what's happened post acceptance?

- No show for the first day of work
- Car accident the day before their first day of work
- Declined the offer at midnight the night before because they were moving out of the country
- Failed background check
- Failed drug screens
- Got lost trying to find the site and decided to quit
- Accepted another job
- Decided to stay at their current employer
- Sent their cousin in to work for them on their first day of work

No Shows, Changing Minds

Some of these seem far-fetched. I'm sorry to report they are not.

I am very pro-candidate so if you get another offer, or your dream job happens to come through, I get it. Take the opportunity! Just let the company that you originally accepted know. Not showing up or declining at midnight while the team and recruiter are fast asleep is not ok.

I understand that companies pull job offers, take a long time to interview, put people through multiple offers, and lay people off. However, how you represent yourself is your brand and your image, and we all need to work to live. As I mentioned when we discussed networking, you never know who you're going to meet and who is going to move to the next company. Give the recruiter and hiring manager a heads up that you're taking another offer and keep it professional.

I once had a candidate who called and left me a voicemail at midnight telling me that they wouldn't be showing up the next day for their new job. They had taken a different position, and they were moving out of the country. The candidate absolutely knew that they were accepting another offer for days prior (if not weeks) and called me the Sunday before, at midnight, when they knew I wouldn't be available. They also knew it was unlikely that I would call them back because I'd be scrambling on Monday to cancel their payroll, new employee profile, etc.

They were right.

I didn't have time to call them back, and the manager followed up with them on Tuesday, via email. We had to undo the onboarding process, and re-open the position so we didn't have time to follow up with a candidate who called us at midnight the night before. It was an unfortunate situation when the candidate had actually accepted a counter offer at their current employer, decided to stay, didn't move out of the country, and then found themselves looking to leave again just three months later.

Failed Background Checks and Drug Screens

One would think that this wouldn't happen very often since most people know that this is a standard part of a job search/application process; however, it happens more than you think and at all levels of positions.

Occasionally, if a drug or background check was taking too long to come back, and we didn't want to delay a candidate's start date any further, we'd let a candidate start with these items pending. We'd make them aware of the situation and that the offer was contingent upon clean checks, so if something came back, we'd need to terminate their employment.

Should be ok, right?

Every time that we made the decision to do this and let someone start without these items clear, they failed.

I will never, ever agree to let someone start without these items again. I've learned valuable lessons, and hopefully so did those candidates.

Getting Lost and Doppelgangers

My favorite stories about post acceptance debacles include the new hire who got lost and just gave up, and the one who sent in their cousin on the first day.

I had a new hire who had interviewed at one location, but would be working at another. The locations were less than a mile apart, and they would need to travel between the two locations so it wasn't as strange as it sounds that they didn't see the physical location they were starting at.

The hiring manager called me when the new hire didn't report at 8:30 a.m. for their first day. I called the new hire, who was obviously driving, and in the car.

They were incredibly disgruntled, and said they couldn't find the location and they were giving up. I offered to meet them, tried to give them directions, and tried to help them with their GPS. I had messaged the manager, and they had messaged me back that they would be willing to meet them too. It didn't work though. The new hire hung up on me, and that was the last I heard from them.

I suspect something else was going on because the buildings weren't far apart, weren't hard to get to, and were clearly marked. If I had to guess, they were driving to their other new job, and didn't have any intention of telling us they weren't coming. Just a hunch.

The last story I'll share with you is the case of the doppelganger!

I had a candidate that did an in person, panel interview. They were offered the job and they accepted.

On day one though, we met their cousin.

The person that walked in on day one was clearly not the same person that we interviewed. They were incredibly similar, and if you hadn't spent a considerable amount of time with one of them, you might not have noticed it wasn't the same person.

The candidate who we interviewed was a business analyst. The person who showed up the first day was not.

The person standing in front of me did finally tell me they were a cousin, and that the person who we hired had taken another opportunity and was just trying to help them also get a job.

There are a lot of legal issues that came into play here, but long story short, I sent the cousin home, and we rescinded the offer and backed out the new hire profile in our systems.

This has only happened to me once in my career, but it was shocking. To say I learned a lot is an understatement. Fortunately, this has been a one time situation, and I hope for no repeats!

Chapter 14: The Plot Twist!

I promised a plot twist.

Are you ready for it?

You can read this book. You can search interview tips and tricks online. You can hire a career coach. You can practice interviewing over and over again. Read all the articles and books. Have a referral. Know twelve people who work at the company. Be the best friend of the hiring manager. Be the best employee and interviewer ever. Answer every interview question perfectly. Pass all of the assessments.

And still not get the job.

Through no fault of your own. You could still not get the job.

It hurts and it's frustrating and painful. You are allowed to feel a wave of emotions.

It's not fair. I know it. You know it. Every recruiter and candidate out there knows it. Heck, even hiring managers and teams know it's not fair. However, it's going to happen.

I am not one of those people who will say everything happens for a reason and what's meant to be will be. I hate it when people say that to me, and I know people hate that being said to them when they are looking for a job, and they don't get an offer.

Here is what I will say to you.

I am sorry that this didn't work out for you at this time. Let's look at what we could do differently next time and apply it to our next interview. Sometimes it's out of your control, and there was nothing that you could have done differently. Get mad. Get frustrated. Then redirect yourself, and go back to your career search stronger and wiser.

You are interviewing with people. What I look for may not be what another person looks for. What I'll look past, someone else might not. Something that's a disqualifier for me, might be a non-issue for someone else.

You are dealing with the most unpredictable circumstances when you are job searching. Every person is different from the next. Every recruiter is different. Companies are different, as are their policies and processes. There is so much out of your control.

My advice for everyone in the job market:

- Control what you can control.
- Job searching is a full-time job. Give yourself breaks and time off like you would your day job.
- Give yourself some grace. Can't do it one day? Don't apply. Take a break.
- This is a personal search, but don't take a rejection personally.

- Prepare, do your best, follow up, and keep your head up.
- Applying to hundreds of jobs? Maybe application 201 is the right job. Maybe application 1 is the right job. Stick to quality and follow the process. You will find a job.
- No matter how long it takes to find that right fit, do not get discouraged or get inside your own head. This will just hold you back.

There is a lot of advice out there and searches will give you a hundred different answers on what to do and not to do. Be yourself. Be professional. Be a Unicorn!

You are prepped and ready. Go out there and be your unicorn self. Glitter and sparkle and you'll find the right job for you! You've got this!

Appendix A: The Unicorn Interview Guide

Congratulations! You have an interview lined up!! Here are some guidelines to follow and tips to help you land your next role!

I. **The Top Must Do's!**
   A. Know the position that you applied to and have a copy of the job description in front of you.
      1. Most requests for an interview will come through email and will reference the job that you applied for. If the recruiter/interviewer calls to set up an interview, they should tell you who they are and where they are calling from. Do not get to the phone screen/interview and ask the recruiter or interviewer what job this is for. By the time you get to the scheduled interview, you should know what you are interviewing for.
   B. Be prepared.
      1. Research the company and be able to articulate what they do and some facts that show you looked further than the "About Us" section of the website.

Search for awards that they've received, new products they've launched, news articles on the company, etc.

2. Have questions prepared for the interviewer.

   a) Recruiter: When you're interviewing with the recruiter during a first phone screen interview, have questions prepared about the company and the process. Ask them what they like about the company, what the outlook is for the company, and what they know about the team, etc. Asking recruiters very technical questions about a role won't yield the results that you want — they are in HR and are doing a first assessment of you and your cultural fit, they are not software engineers!

   b) Hiring Manager/Technical Team Member: If you are interviewing with the hiring manager or a technical member of the team, this is the time to ask your detailed questions about the role, expectations, timelines, etc.

C. Dress for the role that you want but also for the company you are interviewing for.

    1. Ask the recruiter what the dress code is for an onsite interview. If you are interviewing for a manufacturing job, and show up to an interview in a suit or high heels, you may not be able to tour the manufacturing floor! (This happened to me personally!) The recruiter will be able to give you a guideline for how to dress for an in person interview.

    2. Virtual interviews: Professional dress! Virtual interviews are a new complexity and wearing a hoodie or a t-shirt will make you seem even more casual. Dress up for virtual interviews, always!

D. Follow Ups.

    1. Sending thank you emails to the interviewer goes a long way. It gives you an opportunity to express your interest again and clarify any questions that you

may not have answered completely.

2. Send a thank you note to the recruiter after a phone screen interview. It doesn't happen very often, and managers often ask if the candidates also thanked us!

II. Biggest Mistakes!

A. Being unprepared

1. Not knowing the role, company, interviewer who you're interviewing with will lose you the job.

2. As a recruiter, when I ask a candidate what they know about the company and they say, "Not much. What can you tell me?" I'm immediately done with the interview. I give them a high level overview and move on with the interview. Very few people have come back from that.

B. Dressing inappropriately/underdressing

1. Ask the recruiter about the dress code before an onsite interview if you're unsure. As mentioned before, dress up for virtual interviews.

C. Talking excessively/tangents/irrelevant answers

1. This is one of the areas that people struggle with the most. Talking at length about your experience will lose your audience. Where this happens the most is during the "Tell us about yourself" question. Practice your high level elevator speech about yourself. This should be no longer than two to three minutes.
2. Highlighting skills that aren't relevant to the role.
    a) A lot of people are particularly proud of certain aspects of their background regardless of whether it fits the role. For example: A military vet highlighted in their phone screen interview that they had a top secret clearance, nine times. The role didn't require a top secret clearance, and the importance of this certification to the candidate was very clear. The role (and the company) didn't require that level of clearance, and the candidate wouldn't

have qualified for the clearance any longer based on the type of work the company did. The candidate was declined before they even had the chance to learn more about the role or company because they highlighted a skill that wasn't necessary, and the interviewer felt that they would be unhappy in losing their clearance. However, had they highlighted their project management skills and training, that would have been relevant, and they would have been moved to the next interview step.

D. Criticizing previous employers/colleagues

1. There are many ways to honestly and professionally say why you are leaving your current employer or why you left a past employer. You will most likely be asked about difficult employees and relationships and how you navigated them. Fight the instinct

to blame employers or
coworkers.
E. Not asking questions
1. A recruiter has valuable insight
into the company. They work with
multiple different groups, teams,
etc. Recruiters typically have
insight into the company's future,
their initiatives and can give their
perspective on the company's
culture. Hiring managers will be
able to lay out expectations,
projects coming up, things that
you could be impactful on right
away. Team members can give
you insight into leadership, daily
operations, and the work
environment.
2. Remember, you are interviewing
the company and the manager as
well. This should be a two way
conversation.

III. **Traditional vs. Behavioral Interviewing**
A. Traditional Interviewing:
1. Traditional interviews are usually
background type questions and
get-to-know-you questions. The
interviewer is looking for a
specific answer from you.
2. Examples include:

a) Tell me about yourself.
b) What were your responsibilities in X role?
c) Why are you interested in this role/company?
d) What are your strengths and weaknesses?
e) Why should we hire you?

B. Behavioral Interviewing:
1. Behavioral interviewing is looking to predict your future behavior (and success) based on your past actions and behaviors. The interviewer is looking for creative thinking, analytical skills, logical thinking, and the ability to learn and adapt.
2. Examples Include:
a) Tell me about a time when you had to meet a difficult timeline.
b) Tell me about a time when you disagreed with your boss.
c) Tell me about a time when you made a mistake.
d) Give me an example of a time when you had a difficult decision to make.

IV. Behavioral Interviewing: STAR Method

A. Situation: Explain the situation to the interviewer. They don't need to know every detail!
B. Task: What the assignment was, what was involved? What was the problem or challenge that you were responsible for?
C. Action: What did you do? What did the team do?
D. Result: What was the outcome? Highlight quantifiable results, what you learned, what you would do differently next time.

V. **Next Steps: Questions to Practice and Prepare For**
   A. Traditional Interview Questions
      1. Tell me about yourself.
      2. What is your favorite part of your current job? What do you not like about your job?
      3. Why are you looking for a new role?
      4. Where did you go to school?
      5. Where do you see yourself in X amount of years?
      6. What is your dream job?
      7. What would you change about your career/job/company?
      8. What are your strengths and weaknesses?

9. What are your salary requirements/expectations?
10. Why should we hire you?
B. Behavioral Interview Questions
   1. How have you handled setbacks?
   2. Share a time when you had to deal with a difficult customer.
   3. How do you handle your schedule when it is interrupted?
   4. Give me an example of how you have communicated with previous managers/team members.
   5. Can you share an example of a time when you were unable to get your point across effectively? What contributed to the issue and how have you improved?
   6. Give an example of a time when you needed information from a coworker who wasn't responsive. What did you do?
   7. Tell me about a time when your coworkers disagreed with you. How did you handle the situation?
   8. Describe a time when you did everything you could think of, but still didn't achieve your desired result. What happened and why

were you unsuccessful? What did you learn?

9. Can you describe a time when you followed a rule that you didn't agree with? Why did you follow it?

10. Tell me about a time when a project's priorities had to change. Explain the steps you took to start the change.